The Product is Docs

Writing technical documentation in a product development group

Christopher Gales and the Splunk Documentation Team

Table of Contents

1. Introduction

Why does this book exist?

In the course of doing our work, the Splunk documentation team strives to adopt (and adapt) industry best practices whenever we can find them, and when we can't, we make every effort to develop them.

There is a substantial body of professional literature on the content itself, including content strategy, user and task analysis, and the right way to design and structure technical information. On the project management side, JoAnn Hackos's pioneering book *Managing your Documentation Projects* is still a keystone work, but it was written and published before the Agile Manifesto transformed the world of software development. Her subsequent *Information Development: Managing Your Documentation Projects, Portfolio, and People* does provide an update for Agile, but it focuses exclusively on the technical communications manager, and it is out of print.

There are articles and conference presentations galore about many aspects of our work as information developers and managers of documentation teams, but in developing our own internal practices, we have found numerous gaps. When we went to create some audience definitions, to our surprise we found that there were no good models to follow specifically for technical documentation. There is a lot of material about persona development for user experience teams, and audience definition for marketing purposes, but nothing for technical documentation, even though every doc team in the world discusses audience all the time.

Similarly, there is a lot of good material about working with subject matter experts in engineering, or teaming with UX, but a lot less about working with QA, customer support, or product management, which are all groups that play a significant role in our daily work.

The more we thought about it, the more the list of underrepresented topics grew. And even for topics that had significant published resources (doing documentation in an Agile environment, collaborative authoring, working with remote teams, and others), we couldn't find anything that felt current and accurately reflected our daily working practices. We wanted a book that covered the reality of developing technical documentation in a fast-moving product development organization, and we discovered that the book we wanted didn't exist.

We kicked off the writing effort as a hack week project, with most of the Splunk doc team contributing messy rough drafts in an effort to capture as much of our thinking as we could in the shortest possible amount of time. From that initial 90 pages, we worked in twos and threes to expand the content and fill out those preliminary thoughts until the rough draft more closely resembled the book you are holding today. Then we took a couple of individual passes through the entire manuscript, followed by a final round of team read-throughs and minor revisions. It took us over a year to write it, with collaboration as our guiding principle throughout the process.

Who is it for?

This book is for you! It is unlikely you would have picked it up and read this far if you weren't interested in it. Perhaps you are a technical writer in a small, high-growth company that is figuring out its processes. Perhaps you are an information-development manager in a large enterprise company with an expanding product line and an ever more complex matrix of cross-functional dependencies. You might work at a medium-sized company where your management is asking you to do more with fewer people, and you want some additional perspective that will help you find a leaner and more effective way to deliver what your business demands. Or you might work outside the technical documentation world, in another part of product development, and are wondering how to collaborate most effectively with the documentation team.

If you work as an information developer, a manager in a documentation team, or in another part of product development that collaborates with the doc team, there is information in this book for you.

What this book isn't

This book is not a complete how-to guide or a deeply detailed prescription for information development in the 21st century.

Nor is this book a work of scholarship. We did research the way you do research when you need to find something out at work: a combination of internet searches, talking to trusted colleagues, and surveying valued conference proceedings and periodicals. If that gave us relevant resources, we used them. If not, we tried to fill the gap based on our own collective intelligence and experience.

What this book is

This book provides a broad perspective about the essential aspects of creating technical documentation in today's product development world. It is a book of opinions and guidance, collected as short essays. We organized the chapters alphabetically, because there is no necessary sequence to the content. You can read selectively about subjects that interest you, or you can read the entire collection in any order you like. Information development is a multidimensional discipline, and it is easy to theorize. We have written this book from our direct experience, using the concrete insights and practices we apply to our work every day. Its purpose is to provoke discussion, shine light on some murky areas, and—we hope—inspire our colleagues to consider their processes and assumptions with new eyes.

2. Agile

Introduction

There is the textbook version of implementing Agile methodology, and then there is the reality. The vast majority of software development teams are using some form of Agile, usually scrum; what they have adopted is a limited or modified version of it.

So what does it mean to be Agile? Let's start with the key components to the Agile Manifesto:

1. **Individuals and interactions** over processes and tools
2. **Working software** over comprehensive documentation
3. **Customer collaboration** over contract negotiation
4. **Responding to change** over following a plan

Sounds straightforward enough. But for the tech writer, what do these principles specifically mean?

Let's discuss each of the Agile Manifesto components and how they apply to the tech writer.

Individuals and interactions

In an Agile environment, you need to be a proactive self-starter, and adaptable. Most of the other scrum team members will not habitually think of reaching out to the documentation team to notify you that a feature or enhancement has a documentation impact. You need to watch for and track down the information.

Ideally, it is best if you can physically work at the same location as other members of your scrum team. Face-to-face interactions are more productive. You can walk across a room or down the hall to talk to your team members for quick discussions. If you are not co-located with your scrum team, see Chapter 20, "Working with Remote Teams."

In addition to attending scrum meetings, there are other steps you can take to keep up with the issues that your scrum team is dealing with.

- Make sure you have access to any chat rooms that your scrum team uses, and track the conversations in those chat rooms.
- Ask to be included on any email distribution lists for your scrum team.
- Watch the Agile boards in whatever tracking tool your team uses.
- Attend standups and exercise your status as a full member of the team.

The more you learn about (and keep on top of) issues and requirements that originate through the more fluid and iterative scrum process, the better prepared you will be to write in an Agile environment.

Working software

The Agile Manifesto says "Working software over comprehensive documentation." Most tech writers pride themselves on their commitment to comprehensive documentation. The balance between *comprehensive* and *relevant* is important for every writer to consider, but that is a separate subject from anything the Agile Manifesto seeks to address.[1]

This part of the Agile Manifesto is commonly misunderstood. "Working software over comprehensive documentation" is not about customer documentation at all. What the Manifesto means is that it is more useful to have working software than it is to have detailed engineering specifications. Creating detailed design specifications at the beginning of a project and then building a product that tightly adheres to those original specs represents an

---

[1] See *Developing Quality Technical Information: A Handbook for Writers and Editors*, Third Edition, Michelle Carey et. al., IBM Press, 2014, 115-149.

older engineering methodology. Such specifications consumed countless hours of time at the beginning of a development cycle, delayed the actual start of software development, and were (sometimes, rarely) updated at the end of the development cycle. Most important, they inhibited adjustments to the design and implementation during the course of development.

Having some engineering specification is actually essential, especially as it relates to intellectual property. These documents are valuable to anchor engineering conversations and to help other groups such as QA, Marketing, Sales, Support, and Docs prepare for a release. However, those internal design documents should also be developed using the Agile process and updated regularly throughout the development cycle.

A scrum team should consider the customer documentation as an integral part of what "working software" means. You, as the documentation writer and customer advocate, will probably need to explain this to your organization. More than once. There is no definition of done without docs. Customer documentation is part of the working software.

Customer collaboration

A regular customer feedback loop is fundamental to the Agile method. Iterative development without constant customer validation isn't really Agile.

You have multiple opportunities to collaborate with customers, including chat rooms, user groups, online forums, conferences, and direct feedback. In addition, you can collaborate with internal customers such as Professional Services and Customer Support, who often have a great perspective on what your customers want. You should also get involved in usability studies and other user research activities that your User Experience team arranges.

You do not need a formal customer feedback program to achieve effective and actionable collaboration. See Chapter 5, "Customer Feedback," for more information.

Responding to change

Quick responses to change are essential. Working in an Agile environment requires continuous development, including continuous documentation development. Change is inevitable. In an Agile environment, especially as a technical writer, you have to have a high tolerance for ambiguity and be ready to adapt to a lot of changes in direction.

It used to be common to have a comprehensive set of plans for each feature in a release. With Agile, there is planning without the need to have detailed, comprehensive plans before work begins. Typically, a framework for a feature is all that is necessary to get started with research tasks and initial development. Then, as development continues, you share incremental progress with select customers and adjust your plans in response to their feedback. If you are working in an integrated scrum team, you can do some of your documentation development in parallel, and make your own adjustments based on customer feedback as the software evolves.

If you are new to the Agile process, keep in mind that adopting Agile is itself a significant change process. It can take some time for an organization to fully embrace the Agile mindset and methodologies. Initially there will be a large number of experiments and reversals, including changing the agreed-on implementation of Agile.

How Agile are you really?

The Agile Manifesto and all of the subsequent discussions and permutations of Agile-like methodologies present an ideal, theoretical picture of software development using Agile methodologies. In reality, there is a lot of variation in how different companies have implemented Agile. Within a company, it also can vary from team to team.

You attend iteration planning meetings, scrum standups, and iteration demo reviews. You read design documents. But if you write your first words about a feature after the development is finished, you are not Agile.

The level of Agile adoption in a company or on a team is almost entirely driven by how well the program management and engineering teams embrace Agile methodologies. See "It's all about the (company) buy-in" in this chapter.

Agile adoption is product-driven

Agile is more applicable to some software development environments than to others. We have identified three distinct environments, based on how the products are delivered to customers.

Cloud or web-only products

Cloud or web-only products are the most successful at implementing and adhering to Agile methodologies. Why? Because typically there is no software for customers to install. Customers use a URL to access the software. Updates to the software can be made at any time without requiring customers to deploy them in on-premises environments. Continuous development and deployment are common practices in cloud services, and well-suited to Agile.

Enterprise or on-premises products

Enterprise or on-prem products are the least successful at fully implementing Agile methodologies. Why? Actually, for several reasons. Probably the most important reason is that customers do not want to continuously update software on their systems. Even a release cadence of every six months can be extremely taxing on IT departments for large complex organizations. This does not mean that organizations that develop enterprise and on-prem products should not use Agile methodologies for software development. But in all likelihood these organizations will implement some sort of variant Agile process, such as Kanban.

The scrums for enterprise or on-prem products tend to be two or three weeks long, with releases every three to six months. Cycles like these are a vast improvement over the annual release cycles that many organizations used to adhere to. Some writers who work on these types of products continue to use more traditional development approaches to writing documentation. We caution you to avoid this tendency when possible. If you rely on a waterfall approach for all your content, you will always be behind your engineering teams, and when you need information from your subject matter experts, they will be sprints beyond the work you are asking them about. Trailing in this way also makes it more difficult for those teams to see you as an integral member and a valued participant in the Agile process. See "How to be more Agile" in this chapter for additional thoughts about doing documentation in scrum environments.

Application or add-on products

Working on small software products with rapid release cycles can be truly challenging for technical writers. You absolutely must be well-organized, relish change, and be able to handle stress.

Here at Splunk, we have some writers who manage 20-70 product releases for new and updated applications every three weeks. Close to the end of the three-week cycle, everyone on the team gets together and determines what is ready to be released. The difficulty with this approach is that it is not easy to find time to make improvements to the documentation that are not part of a specific release. Global improvements like retrievability and navigation, conceptual improvements, or even sustaining improvements to previously released information are hard to plan for, because each individual app or add-on gets updated and released in a single sprint, then waits its turn for the next update sprint.

It's all about the (company) buy-in

If your company is half-hearted about adopting Agile methodologies, you will struggle to be Agile in your information development.

Your success depends on how rigorously the development teams adhere to good Agile practices. The program management team needs to drive the adoption of Agile across the company. They need to model good practices and to provide solid education to all team members. Successful Agile implementations are driven from the top down. This is not a culture change that can be driven by the doc team, or from the bottom up. Individual teams can adopt Agile practices with the participation of only their members, but larger development projects that involve multiple teams require program management leadership.

You can tell how good adoption and buy-in is by looking at the practices of your scrum teams.

- Does your team hold sprint review and planning meetings with all contributing members?
- Does your team open up the tracking tool, such as JIRA or Rally, during those meetings to identify work from the backlog?
- Does your team assign story points to plan their work?
- Does your team embrace or avoid tracking tools? Do they use less structured collaborative tools, such as internal wikis, instead of tools specifically designed for tracking Agile work?
- Is there regular customer feedback flowing in to the development process?

Good Agile practices are not just about holding sprint planning meetings and regular standups. It is also about guiding the teams to adopt the best agile practices for each individual team. We've learned over the years that Agile implementations should not be static. Teams should routinely reevaluate their methodologies to ensure they are working in the most effective way to reach their goals.

How to be more Agile

For technical writers, being Agile is more about relationship-building than anything else.

Have face-to-face interactions as much as possible. Walk across a room or down the hall to talk to your team members for quick discussions. Face-to-face discussions are more productive. An online chat conversation is not the same. With chat, you can type quick, cryptic questions and get the same in return. With email, you can ask three questions and receive responses to two of them, and even those responses aren't necessarily the full answer.

Use your company's standard development tracking program, such as JIRA or Rally, to track your documentation tasks, doc reviews, to raise issues and questions, and to file defects. There are several reasons for this. You are a team member, the same as any developer, UX, or QA team member. Using the same tools as the other team members promotes seamless interaction and provides more visibility into your information development work.

Add story points to the tickets that have documentation impact. There are tasks that require a lot of engineering work and very little documentation work. There are other tasks that require a small or medium amount of engineering work but require a large amount of documentation work. Make your work visible in the same tickets that development uses to organize and track their work.

Push the product managers to write scenario-based user stories. All too often, stories do not provide enough context for meaningful development work. This context is important not just for you, the tech writer, but for everyone from Marketing and Sales, to QA, Support, and Training. Everyone needs to know who the audience is and what they are trying to accomplish with the feature. You might need to push, nag, and cajole your colleagues into writing good user stories, but it is worth the effort. For more discussion about this, specifically from the tech writing perspective, see Chapter 12, "Scenario-driven Information Development."

The definition of done

Engineering teams are anxious to finish their release work so that QA can complete their testing and the work on a feature can be declared "Done." Ideally, in Agile development, "Done" means that engineering, QA, and documentation are all finished with their work and at the end of the sprint, you have developed and tested shippable, documented code. Project managers who strive to keep to this ideal often pressure writers to complete work in the same iteration that engineering completes its work. If the engineers are checking in code up to the very last minute, it is impossible for the writer—or even QA—to complete their work at the same time. It also preempts the team's opportunity to conduct timely technical review of draft material, and the writer's opportunity to revise content to match the software delivery.

In engineering-driven scrums, engineers and project managers often do not include the documentation in the definition of done, because it is too difficult to track docs as an outlying activity. You have to evaluate the kind of scrum team you're on, as well as the specific information you have to develop, before you can decide on what approach you will take to Agile and how closely to tie your work to the software development.

Use scrum for what it's good for

Scrum is so dominant in product development teams today that writers spend a lot of energy and effort figuring out how to integrate with the scrum process. Where you have documentation to develop that is closely tied to a specific, discrete feature, scrum can work really well. In those cases, use it, following the suggestions we have made in this chapter.

But it is important to remember that scrum isn't good for everything. There is plenty of work that is not well-suited to Agile methodology. As a technical writer, you know this firsthand. Consider the following types of content that are typically not tied to a specific scrum team:

- Troubleshooting
- Release notes
- Migration or upgrade information
- End-to-end tutorials
- Best practices
- Some API work

And further consider the following types of documentation activities that lie outside the main flow of product development:

- Persona development
- Learning objectives
- Editing
- Improving existing content
- Responding to customer feedback

If your company is using Agile, or considering switching to Agile, be discerning about the kind of information you deliver to customers. Feel empowered to use the methodology that suits your work best. For the parts of your work that are a good fit with scrum, there's nothing better. For the parts of your work that are not well-suited to scrum, figure out what you need to get from the team during their sprints, how you and the project manager want to track those requests using Agile tools and methods, and then run your own information-development project alongside the scrum teams using whatever project management method works best for you. At Splunk, we have introduced the idea of "Agile checklists," which are a sprintable artifact we can use to collect relevant information within the scrum process so that writers can use it to develop information that spans multiple sprints or scrum teams.

Doc team and scrum participation

Two popular approaches to writing documentation in Agile environments are to have writers participate directly on scrum teams, and to have a separate scrum team of writers that documents the work of the development teams as the work is finalized. Let's call these two models **direct participation** and **scrum of writers**.

Direct participation

Most doc teams use the direct participation approach. With direct participation, you establish the documentation function as a peer to engineering, UX, and QA. The approach improves the standing of the documentation team in the eyes of the other functions.

As you become more and more familiar with a feature or product, you demonstrate the value that you bring to the scrum team in the story planning and task details. You will advocate for the customer for improvements to the UI, for comprehensive API documentation, and for consistency in parameter and attribute naming.

You will be in a position to quickly review error messages, UI text strings, and other localizable files as those items are being developed and coded. This advantage is a key benefit to the direct participation approach, which can preclude misunderstandings by customers and save Customer Support hours of time addressing issues after the product ships.

With direct participation, the subject matter experts and project managers have a single point of contact to speak to for documentation related issues and they can involve you in discussions or meetings that might result in a documentation impact.

This approach also can offer a more satisfying, inclusive team experience for you as a writer. You identify closely with your users and want those users to succeed. As you become an integral part of the scrum team, other scrum team members will proactively seek out your opinion.

While the direct participation approach can foster deep product knowledge in specific areas, which is good, it can lead to silos and an inability to share writing resources across different scrums. Writers can't necessarily fill in for each other during absences or help each other if a particular feature area sees a spike in activity. You can mitigate this by designating backup writers for each area, or by periodically moving writers to different product areas to gain knowledge of other parts of the product.

Also, as the engineering team grows faster than the documentation team in sheer numbers of people, the number of scrum teams will increase. Writers will likely need to participate in multiple scrum teams. As more and more scrum teams form, this can be very taxing on the doc team. This situation can be exacerbated by the fact that not all writers will have the knowledge to cover any new scrum that is formed.

Finally, it can be harder for you to communicate the work that is happening in your individual scrum teams to other writers whose work might be affected. It can be more difficult to ensure that each writer sees the big picture of a release and can identify areas of possible gaps or overlaps in your work.

Scrum of writers

Setting up a separate scrum team and sprint cadence for writers separate from the rest of product development is not a true Agile approach. Being involved with the scrum team only late in the development cycle means that you invest less time tracking ongoing changes as features evolve and change. When you begin to write, the feature is likely to be close to its final state. With a scrum of writers, there are good opportunities for cross-training.

Over time, as you learn multiple areas of the product, the writers form a team who can fill in for each other during absences or work together on a particular feature area that has a peak in activity during a particular release.

Additionally, subject matter experts always know to go to a specific point person, the manager of the scrum of writers, with any questions they have about documentation resourcing or to request documentation support for new efforts.

As with the direct participation approach, there are challenges to the scrum of writers approach. The most significant challenge is being involved late in the development cycle, which means that writers do not have opportunities to influence the design of the product or feature to make it more useful or usable. Not having these types of early input from writers can result in needing more written documentation than would otherwise have been required. Additionally, the lack of writer participation in the development cycle can also lead to inconsistent UI designs, naming conventions, and poorly worded error messages, all of which will ship as product defects if it is too late to change them.

Less direct involvement means that you are less likely to hear about changes in scope or functionality that might be communicated informally only among the scrum team. Consider how mature your organization's product development process is and whether the writers can count on getting the information that they need if they are not part of the scrum team.

Also, if a pool of writers contributes to different parts of the documentation for a feature, the resulting output might have inconsistencies that range from different writing styles to conflicting facts.

Finally, using a separate scrum of writers violates most of the tenets of the Agile Manifesto, and usually results in a more waterfall approach masquerading as iterative development. If you find yourself considering the scrum of writers, consider that scrum might not be the best methodology for those tasks, and you might not need to use it at all to achieve efficient and effective results.

Number and size of scrum teams

Scrum teams are often organized primarily based on the working needs of software developers, with other cross-functional areas slotted in afterwards. Work with your program management office to establish a good process for forming and starting a scrum team. Without such a process, there is a strong chance that writers will have to cover more scrum teams than they should. If you are participating as a writer on more than two scrum teams, that's a strong sign that the way your organization institutes scrum teams needs some adjustment.

Scrum teams should also remain small. Large teams, or a large number of products assigned to one team, become unwieldy in Agile. It is difficult to get everyone to show up for standups if the team is too large. You don't get status or blockers from everyone on a regular basis. Agile works best in teams of 10 or fewer, including development, product management, UX, QA, docs, and a scrum master. If you are on a large team trying to do scrum, talk to your program manager about breaking the team up into several smaller teams.

Inconsistencies across scrum teams

Because software developers tend to work on a single scrum team, inconsistencies can occur in the UI, in messages, and on naming conventions across teams. While your UX team or PM team should be tracking the standards, these inconsistencies often fall through the cracks. QA and doc team members are in a unique position to identify and call attention to these inconsistencies because these team members typically work on multiple scrum teams.

The full circle

Every tech writer knows two basic things about our work:

- We spend only a fraction of our time actually writing.
- The information development cycle is circular and continuous.

When we explain this to scrum teams, we use a graphic like this:

The information development cycle resembles the software development cycle in some ways, and it is worth educating your scrum team about how your work flows, what its cadence is, and what the inputs and outputs are. The more you can illuminate your mental model to them and highlight the contact points, the more successful your engagement with the scrum team will be, and the more successful the overall scrum team will be in achieving its goals.

3. Audience

As technical writers, we talk a lot about audience. Most writers pride themselves on knowing who they are writing for and advocating for the customer within the product development team. Most writers also write from a vaguely-defined, intuitive sense of who their audience is. Let's be clear: these writers are highly informed, and often directly in touch with actual customers, so they are not basing their decisions on imagination or fantasy. But it is a rare doc team that has developed concrete audience definitions and based their content on them.

We consider there to be an important difference between an audience definition and a persona. Many teams use personas to guide their design and development decisions. But a persona is a *concrete characterization*, rather than a well-defined *audience type*. Both are valuable, but they are not the same.

Reliable and accessible documentation requires thorough product knowledge. It also depends equally, if not more, on knowing your audience.

Technical writers craft connections between an audience and a product. To build these connections, you need to identify your users as clearly as possible. You also need to identify your users' goals: the problems that they want to solve, the decisions that they need to make, or the things that they want to build. Equipped with this audience awareness, you can write more accessible, well-situated, and supportive documentation. You can also help create more satisfied customers.

How identifying audience can help a documentation team

Your documentation audience is likely made up of users with different experience levels, business roles, or use cases. You might be surprised to find out how many different audiences use your content. Moving towards a clearer and more nuanced sense of who is reading your documentation can help teams and individual writers in many ways, from figuring out team responsibilities to information architecture and all the way down to editing a sentence.

Here are some areas where audience analysis and understanding can help you and your team.

Team structure, expertise, and responsibilities

Knowing your audience can help the team decide which writers to recruit or to hire. Understanding the customers that you serve helps you identify the areas of expertise or experience you should seek when you are hiring.

Audience analysis can also help to identify learning opportunities for current team members. Writers might need to become more familiar with a certain kind of use case, external developer framework, or some aspect of the company's product line in order to better serve the users consulting the docs.

Audience can also play an important role when you are determining how to assign information development work. Certain writers might have particular familiarity with specific sections of the audience, such as app developers, data analysts, or system administrators, which will make them better suited to shape documentation structure and content for these users.

User testing and feedback

Your team might also conduct documentation user testing. Understanding your audience can help with identifying representative users to provide feedback on the docs.

User feedback can provide other important audience insights. Comments or questions can highlight particular use cases, business roles, or areas of interest among your readers.

Delivery format

Knowing your audience can influence the publication or delivery format for your team's documentation. Your audience might comprise users who prefer online documentation, users who prefer printed versions, or both. Making a printable option available can make online documentation more accessible for all users.

If your team creates online documentation, audience awareness can also help with determining whether the user interface and other aspects of the online format suit users' needs. Are users satisfied with the available options for navigating, searching, and reading the docs? If your audience includes users who consume the docs on desktop computers and mobile devices, is your content accessible and correctly formatted for both platforms?

Information architecture and learning objectives

Identifying your audience helps you to focus your writing and lets you craft content that is appropriately scoped and detailed.

When trying to evaluate the level of detail for your audience, consider the following.

- Do the details you provide match the audience's average experience level?
- Does the content provide *too much* detail for this audience?

You can also use audience insights to help you decide on content organization, either online or in a manual. As part of assessing content organization, your team might ask the following questions.

- How can we best organize our content on a website or within a manual to cater to our audience and how it prefers to learn?
- How should topics relate to each other? Does our audience strictly prefer one-stop information lookup and retrieval, or are they amenable to delving into a subject and reading a series of comprehensive topics?

- Does our audience need links to other relevant topics peppered throughout topics, or just at the end?
- Does each topic need to tell a single "story" (describe a single use case or focus on a particular feature or component) or can it tell multiple stories?

Chapter 8, "Learning Objectives," provides more details on defining and using learning objectives to craft content for a particular audience.

Content structure and formatting

Last, but not least, audience awareness can help you with even the finest of content details, including sentence length and word choice. With your audience in mind, consider the following questions when you review content.

- How many sections should a topic have?
- How long should each paragraph be?
- Are sentence length and structure appropriate?
- Is your audience familiar with the terminology that you are using?
- Should you define terms in each topic where they appear or just once in an introductory section?
- Is content accessible and appropriate for an international audience?
- If your team works with translators, can your content be localized easily?

Putting the picture together: audience definition resources

How do you figure out who is reading your documentation? Putting together a clear picture of your audience can seem like a daunting prospect. Experience helps, as you will naturally develop and refine a sense of your users over time. For any writer, however, there are resources that can help you get started and keep you thinking about audience throughout the information-development process.

Start with available audience information

Your documentation team might already have an audience definition or reference. If you have not heard about one yet, ask your manager or colleagues if one exists. Even if the audience definition is a bit dated, it can be a useful foundation. Knowing a bit of product history can help you identify "veteran" users and newer users in your current audience.

If no audience definition is available, you might discuss creating one with your colleagues. Creating audience definitions, whether for some particular area of your company's product line or more generally, should be a collaborative process.

If your team decides to create audience definitions, see "Defining an audience: a case study" in this chapter for an example of how to approach this task.

Use internal documentation to gain insight

When you are working on a specific project or feature, start to analyze your audience early. You can often find valuable audience information in a product manager's spec or requirements document about the feature. Product managers often provide notes on who will most likely use a new feature or who has requested an enhancement. They also often provide notes about typical or anticipated use cases and benefits. If this kind of information is not available at the outset of a documentation project, ask your team's product manager about it.

Learn from colleagues who (also) work with users

As a technical writer, you might have some level of regular user interaction yourself. You also have colleagues who work with users and who can help you understand and anticipate audience and use cases for a particular feature. Talk to your team's product manager about new and existing features. Get to know user experience designers and researchers, support engineers, customer education specialists, and anyone else who talks to users on a regular basis.

Communicate with users

Direct user feedback can provide valuable information about who is using your company's products and who is reading the docs. You might regularly respond to user feedback or questions as part of your technical writing work. Feedback can give you an idea of use cases, typical areas of interest or confusion, experience levels. Occasionally, responding to a comment or other feedback can be an opportunity to conduct a (judiciously limited) bit of user research. If it seems appropriate and a user is willing to discuss their question(s) or comments further, you can sometimes gain information about how and which customers are using a product.

In addition to feedback, you might have the opportunity to participate in community forums, chat rooms, or other user group activities. Reach out when you can and share the insights you gain with your colleagues.

Additional resources

Other chapters in this book offer more detailed advice that can help you with thinking about and creating audience definitions. For more information, see the following chapters.

- 5, "Customer Feedback"
- 8, "Learning Objectives"
- 9, "Maintaining Existing Content"
- 12, "Scenario-driven Information Development"
- 19, "Working with Product Management"
- 21, "Working with User Experience and Design"

Defining an audience: a case study

This section gives you an idea of how the Splunk documentation team analyzed and created a set of audience definitions.

When we started to talk about audience definitions in the Splunk doc team, we did some research to see what other doc teams had done. We found something interesting, which was that we found almost nothing at all. There is a lot of persona work available from UX teams, and user and task analysis from doc teams, and audience analysis from marketing teams. There are also a lot of presentations and articles that talk about how writers should think about audience. But we really didn't find any meaningful, specific examples of audience definitions for technical documentation.

At this point you might be saying to yourself that your UX or product team, or even the technical writers themselves, have a set of carefully-crafted personas to guide information development work. If that's the case, great! Personas, especially when grounded in user and task analysis, are an excellent tool for documentarians. But a persona definition and an audience definition are not the same thing.

Here is an example of a Splunk doc team audience definition:

Admin 1

Entry-level admin audience, mainly admins whose experience is limited to installing and running a single Splunk platform instance. Can follow directions while utilizing a CLI (running commands and directory navigation,) and has a basic understanding of TCP ports. Understands what a universal forwarder is, and how to use it. Can follow basic data ingest tasks. Can install an app or add-on via the GUI. Has basic data structure awareness, such as timestamps. Understands how to get data to an index. Can add users.

May not have much Splunk experience from the Analyst/Knowledge Manager perspective. Theoretical aspirations of a typical member of the described audience: Install and run a single-instance Splunk deployment. Understand what a universal forwarder is, and how to use it. Perform basic data ingest tasks. Install an add-on or app via CLI. Basic data structure awareness, such as time stamps. How to get data to an index. Search command syntax for formatting data and basic stats output. How to add users. Intro to alerting.

A persona should certainly align with an audience definition. But a persona is a specific instance of someone who belongs to an audience type. There might be an Admin 1 persona named Maria, who works at a company of a specific size, and who is a Windows administrator whose boss is asking her to spend more time building dashboards, even though most of what she knows about the Splunk platform pertains to the indexing tier. A persona like that tells you how an individual person in a particular context will use the product. It guides feature development, and is interesting for the doc team to consider. But our experience indicates that a useful audience definition works better than a persona for training new writers, applying techniques like learning objectives, guiding broader information design and development questions, and enabling customers to identify what content is relevant to them.

So how do you formulate an audience definition? Ideally, it's a team process that turns the informed intuition of writers into a clear, concrete summary that pins down that vague idea they have carried in their heads for so long. The inputs to the discussion come from customer contact, UX research, product management guidance, and writer experience. The difficult part is finding the balance of reaching something generic enough to apply broadly but focused enough to be useful for writers working on specific topics.

When we did the exercise at Splunk, we convened a short-term project team of seven writers whose expertise spanned the product portfolio. They had weekly meetings for five weeks. Their discussion started by sharing, in writing, their assumptions about who they were writing for, then identifying any important audiences that weren't represented. Then they worked out the right level of detail to use for the definitions. For example, is a security analyst a separate audience, or could we have just one audience definition for all kinds of IT analysts? Wherever possible, we favored a more generic definition. Our group also realized that for some audiences (specifically administrator and developer), we needed more than one level, because the customer's knowledge and experience significantly affected the kind of content we would write for them. With those boundaries established, the team created an information model of what an audience definition should include, then turned to a typical cycle of draft-review-revise to finalize the definitions. When they were confident that they had created useful guidance for the rest of their colleagues, we rolled them out to the entire doc team. We also shared them with the UX and product management teams, in the effort to create shared vocabulary and understanding about who we are writing docs—and building products—for.

What we learned

At the end of this comprehensive audience analysis, the team had a set of audience definitions with considerable detail on each user category and sub-category. Generally, the following considerations helped us the most in clarifying our audience definition.

- **Audience types:** You can base audiences on business roles or titles, as we did, or something else that makes sense for your company. For example, if your user experience department already has a list of user personae for your product, this might give your team some food for thought. Remember the differences between a user persona and an audience definition.

- **Audience levels:** We added experience and/or capability levels to many audience types, such as "Admin 1" and "Dev 2."

We tried to be very deliberate when doing so, including concrete details about what sets one level apart from the next. Typical use cases and skill or experience levels in external areas (such as programming languages) can be helpful in distinguishing one level from another. You might not have multiple levels within a particular audience type, so don't force these distinctions, but be open to them if they are helpful.

- **Audience attributes:** We added attributes to each user category and sub-category to help further specify the experience levels, business roles, and use cases that distinguish each one. In our case, some of the most helpful attributes were specific to our product or software. For example, we defined skill levels for the Splunk Search Processing Language in order to clarify the experience and capabilities of various audience types and levels.

While the audience analysis has clear benefits for new writers during their training, it was also illuminating for current writers. Audience definitions help writers re-evaluate existing content and move more easily from one assignment to another. Furthermore, a documentation team can share audience definitions with other groups within the company, including software engineers, sales and marketing, customer education, support, and user experience. It can be useful to compare notes and see if different departments share similar ideas about who is using the company's product.

Ultimately, it is useful for a documentation team to revisit audience definitions and assumptions regularly. Be open to having accepted ideas challenged or expanded both when your team investigates or analyzes audience and at any moment. Users can offer valuable insight into your audience at any time–feedback, community forums, and user group meetings can help your insight evolve.

4. Collaborative Authoring

Technical writing always requires some degree of collaborative authoring. This might mean extensively reviewing and possibly repurposing engineering documents or community forum posts, or it might mean working directly with another writer on shared content.

Writers who have been working in the industry for some years have probably experienced the shift from the information development model where single authors own single manuals to more collaborative models involving component content management systems, source control, and collaboration platforms such as wikis.

Writers who are just entering the profession have grown up as natives of the web, accustomed to topic-level content organization and the prevalence of search. They were also raised in an educational system that emphasizes collaboration and group projects.

Agile software methodologies include a stronger team focus in the overall sprint process, as well as techniques like pair programming. These principles are also influencing information development practices. The combination of tools, education, and industry trends pushes us ever more strongly towards a true collaborative authoring model.

At Splunk, technical writers tend to own specific areas of the product, which can overlap with other writers, depending on customer workflows and the structure of our information set. In some cases, writers work closely together on shared deliverables. In other cases, writers coordinate their work to ensure consistency and relevance. And in other cases, writers collaborate with technical subject matter experts to fulfill customer requests and other documentation requirements. In all these cases, it is worth adjusting your practices to produce the best customer result with the most efficient process.

Work with multiple writers

Working with another author can be a fun way to shake things up, get a second perspective on your work, learn new skills, and uncover style variations between writers for the same product. Occasionally it can be frustrating and a challenge to blend varied world views into a single document. Either way, here are a few tips for successful and happy co-writing.

- Get an editor.
- Use your company style guide. A company style guide should create enough consistency that personal style habits are not jarring to a reader. If you don't have a company style guide, make one! In the meantime, you can use the *Google Developer Documentation Style Guide*, the *Microsoft Manual of Style,* or another publicly available style guide to create some alignment. A style guide also helps mediate and resolve style discussions between writers.
- Regularly review other writers' work throughout the writing process. Make sure the information you are producing does not overlap or contradict, either when you work on new features or when you link to another writer's work.
- A formal peer review program help expose you to other writers' work and can promote consistency and shared understanding, which will promote an improved customer experience with your content.
- Read each other's work without an editor's pencil. Make sure you understand what your colleagues are doing (and that you aren't covering the same areas or contradicting each other).
- Let it go. The days when technical writers really owned their material are over. Nothing is "all yours." You are working in a team environment, and whether or not you are collaborating directly, assignments are fluid and what you work on today someone else might pick up next month. Remember to be flexible in your personal preferences in order to compromise with other

writers. Keep the shared goal in mind: you are building a cohesive product.

- If a collaboration persists through multiple units of work, then get outside reviews, edits, and feedback.

Work with technical authors

Some subject matter experts (SMEs) are more vested than others in the final documentation product, and they provide extensive raw material for you to work with. They can also have strong ideas and opinions about how the final content should look. When working with very doc-involved SMEs, here are some tips:

- Be prepared to (patiently and cheerfully) explain the reasoning behind your edits and reorganization.
- Listen to their feedback. If you decide not to act on part or all of it, be prepared to explain the clear reasons why not.
- In some cases, you might decide that adhering to every rule in your company's style guide to the letter is less important than encouraging a knowledgeable SME who is interested in documentation to continue his or her engagement with the doc team. Keep your management in the loop if you are departing from standards, and let the SME know that you are acceding, but that you want to evolve the content over time to bring it into alignment.

How wide should a collaboration be?

Most modern authoring tools allow for collaborative writing. At Splunk, we write most of our docs in a wiki-based system, and any employee can edit the docs. The documentation team has additional permissions for creating topics and reorganizing content, but any employee can make text changes within a topic. This level of openness has pros and cons, and it can be an adjustment for writers who are used to working in more closed systems, including desktop publishing and DITA-based environments.

The low barrier to participation encourages internal users to engage with the doc process, report problems, and share a sense of ownership in the published product. It also provides a feedback mechanism that you can use for technical reviews, where the reviewer can work directly in the same system you use.

On the other hand, when any employee can edit the docs, they can introduce incorrect or redundant information. They can also contribute information that does not consider its context, is confusingly written, or tells only part of the story. At Splunk, the doc team uses RSS readers to monitor edits to customer-facing content and to review those changes. And while any employee *can* edit Splunk documentation, the reality is that very few of them actually *do*. Out of that comparatively small number, the majority are well-informed and edit responsibly. There are only two or three instances a year where we need to roll back a contribution from outside the doc team. For us, the advantages outweigh the disadvantages.

Examples

The following table lists some examples of collaborative authoring, with some key points highlighted.

Example	Collaboration model	Key points
Administrator guidance	Coordinated by one writer with multiple contributing writers	• Contributing writers might also need to adjust other topics they own elsewhere. • Ensure that terminology and style are consistent. • Writers should review any content that they link to.

Example	Collaboration model	Key points
		• Establish clear ownership for sustaining work and addressing customer feedback.
Troubleshooting topics	Coordinated by one writer with multiple contributing SMEs	• Communicate solid reasons for the changes you make. • Make the SMEs feel valued. • Determine when striving for consistent style interferes with developing useful information.
"Superfriends"	Ongoing content development group of SMEs and writers	• Work flexibly so SMEs don't have to change their development practices. • Value the time the SMEs spend. • Derive clear requirements and tasks to implement SME suggestions.
This book	Multiple authors working in parallel	• Establish clear assignments and

Example	Collaboration model	Key points
		deadlines. • Use a peer review process. • Use an editor to ensure a consistent level of detail and terminology.

Working with editors

If you work with technical editors, you add another layer of collaboration. The previous sections emphasized the value that editors can bring to a collaborative authoring environment by ensuring consistency, adherence to style, correct terminology, and a focus on lean content. Interactions with editors are also collaborative authoring in their own right. See Chapter 13, "Technical Editing" for a complete discussion of the writer/editor collaboration.

5. Customer Feedback

An open and active customer community is essential in today's crowded software and services environment. Offering and actively managing customer interaction gives you the opportunity to engage in an ongoing conversation with the people who are actually using your products and documentation. By doing so, you gain immediate, valuable insight into whether or not your documentation is achieving its goals. Many companies have begun inviting their customers and clients to influence the overall product direction as well as provide specific feedback through support cases and surveys.

For software documentation, it can be as simple as setting up feedback form on your documentation website that forwards email to a documentation team email alias. Ideally, you should include a way for you to respond to customers that send feedback; for example, by having them fill out an email address field on the website feedback form, or a database to look up an email address if the customer has logged in to your web site.

Customers who have taken the time to submit documentation feedback appreciate it when a writer responds, even if the feedback was negative. Any feedback mechanism that you install must result in action. Customers need to know that the company will acknowledge and respond to any concerns or suggestions that they raise through the form.

It is also important to respond promptly to feedback you receive. If a customer doesn't get a response within the first 72 hours, trends have shown that it is likely that they will not ever receive it. Splunk documentation team members usually respond to feedback within 48 hours, even if it is only to acknowledge the comment and tell the customer that we need time for additional research in order to provide an answer. We try never to let customer feedback sit unaddressed for more than three days.

Splunk has developed and fostered a sense of community with its customers from the beginning. As the company grows and more people use Splunk software, the amount of feedback has increased, as has the need to maintain close ties with the company's most vocal customers. The Splunk documentation team conducts over 50 customer conversations per week, mostly through direct feedback on the documentation pages. This ongoing customer conversation is essential to the Splunk documentation "brand." It helps power the Splunk community, and continuously improves the experience of Splunk customers with our products and the company.

Being responsive and attentive to customer feedback has helped Splunk establish a great sense of community within its user base, as well as providing us with countless opportunities to improve our documentation in tangible, specific ways.

How to collect customer feedback

There are a variety of methods you can use to gather customer feedback, ranging from social media to feedback forms on your documentation web site to surveys at user conferences to formal user research and usability testing. Different organizations have different degrees of barriers between documentation teams and customers. Find the path of least resistance and take it. The important thing is to start the conversation and then make sure you continue it.

Within your company, there will be other groups and programs involved in the customer conversation. If you have a user experience team, coordinate with them so you can participate in usability testing. Keep the UX team in the loop when you discover workflows that are difficult to document, file defects that ask for improvement, and use those observations to frame usability testing sessions.

If your product management or program management team are coordinating beta programs or other preview activities, ensure that the documentation team is represented in the participant meetings. Add your questions to the ongoing beta surveys and make iterative improvements to your content based on the responses.

If your company does formal surveys, like customer satisfaction or net promoter score, there can be some value to collecting documentation-related metrics as part of that program. It is more valuable, though, to collect specific feedback and maintain an ongoing conversation with your customers. Surveys that run only a few times a year will not give you the tangible, actionable feedback you need to improve your content. They also tend to be an extreme lagging indicator. It will take several survey cycles before improvements you make are reflected in general survey results. It is much better to get pointed feedback from an individual, address it, validate the change with that person, and move on with the knowledge that this specific improvement will benefit other customers.

Working with frustrated customers

Sometimes you will hear from customers who are frustrated by how your product does or does not behave, or how your documentation does or does not describe how to use the product. Anyone who has worked in customer service has had to deal with an irate or frustrated customer. In the case of documentation, the ire mostly stems from inadequate or incomplete documentation. Most of the time, frustrated users of the Splunk documentation want to complete a task or install a product and cannot because the instructions assume a certain level of experience and do not account for novices, or because they can't find the information they need.

Also, a lack of organization can cause customers to become sour. Some documentation can be frustrating because writers have not presented it in a way that coincides well with how the product actually works, or with the customer's mental model and terminology.

The key takeaway is that the negative feedback is almost never about the documentation writer personally. If you receive negative feedback as a documentation writer, take it seriously, but don't take it personally. Instead, follow these pointers when dealing with an irate customer:

- When you reply, acknowledge their frustration. You won't fully understand what is upsetting them so much, but starting with a sympathetic tone oftentimes helps cool down the situation rapidly.

- Make a direct offer to assist where able. People are frustrated because they can't do something they expect to do fairly easily. In many occasions, they just want to do the thing in front of them so that they can move to the next thing. Acknowledge their frustration, then give them a path to the result they want. For example, say in your reply: "If you could give me a bit more information about what you were trying to do and how this topic could be more helpful, I can steer you in the right direction and then I will revise the topic to make it better."

- Remain in contact. If a customer doesn't respond after you send a response, follow up again. Provide a customer with the opportunity to continue (or end) the conversation.

- Evaluate whether the feedback is something you can take direct action on or if it needs additional research. Some feedback you can answer right away. Others require coordinating with the engineering or support teams, filing a defect or support case, or publishing in a community forum (such as the Splunk Answers site). Tell the customer in your feedback response the action you plan to take, and keep them updated throughout the process.

- In cases where the customer is asking a question that is highly specific to his or her environment, suggest that the customer post the question to the community forum, or offer to post it for them, so they can benefit from the experience and knowledge of the broader community.

- Be honest with any response. While most companies prohibit disclosure of confidential information such as release dates, or promised fixes for bugs (with a date or not), if there is something about the software or documentation that can be improved, admit it. No one expects products to be perfect. Most customers will appreciate your candor, and it will give them a sense that they are dealing with a company that has integrity.

- On rare occasions, customers can be upset enough that you should not try to address it on your own. Don't be afraid to get others involved, such as your manager, customer support, or the customer's sales representative.

- Sometimes, feedback can be too negative, or the customer is merely being abusive. Back out of such an exchange politely, or don't start a conversation in the first place. Use your judgment to determine when a person is merely frustrated at a bad experience or is just looking for a place to vent and does not expect or want a meaningful exchange.

From customer feedback to company success

As you collect customer feedback and engage in direct conversations with customers, look and listen for patterns that will help you improve your documentation. Are there certain challenges that come up again and again?

- Are entry-level users having a hard time getting started with a task? They might need a workflow topic or improved navigation through the content.

- Are advanced users not finding the detailed information they need? Consider how you are progressively disclosing complexity, and whether your terminology and mental model match theirs.

- Are people asking the same question over again? Make sure you have actually documented it. If you have, analyze why the existing topic is difficult for customers to discover, then update it so that the readers can find it more easily.

Whatever methods you use to collect and respond to customer feedback, communication within the company at all levels is a requirement. A company that instills good communication among all of its departments has a better chance of addressing reactive feedback as well as providing mechanisms for proactive interaction. At Splunk, the documentation, engineering, user experience, support, and education teams often share information and discuss how to address customer problems. Your customers are your biggest asset. In this technical age of social media, they can have a big impact on your company's success. Splunk takes its customers seriously when they provide documentation feedback, and we do our best to address those concerns. This effort has increased positive interactions within the company and between writers and customers. The doc team's continuous customer contact is the fuel in our engine. It has improved product adoption, enhanced the company brand, and established a formidable brand for the documentation team itself.

6. Documenting Third-party Products

Logic suggests that you avoid, at all costs, a situation in which you are delivering technical information about a product that your own company does not develop. Generally, if a product is developed by an organization other than your own, it should not be your responsibility to document that product. Although the reason would appear to be obvious–it doesn't belong to you–there's more to it than that. Documenting a third-party product:

- Adds maintenance burden for an additional product into which you may have limited insight.
- Requires you to keep track of new releases.
- May require you to make substantial unplanned changes at an inconvenient time.
- Might imply a contract of support where there is none.

But what if your customers cannot be successful following a procedure in your own product without also performing some prerequisite or simultaneous procedure in a product with which your product integrates? What if your product doesn't just integrate with a third-party product, but runs on or inside that other product? What if the third-party product's own documentation is insufficient, inaccurate, or out of date? If your documentation's primary directive is to ensure customer success, a blanket statement of never documenting any third-party product technical information might be a disservice to your customers.

In a case where you have determined that you do need to document some element of a third-party product, how you proceed depends on these four factors:

- Availability and accuracy of the third-party product documentation.
- Whether there are required settings or configurations in the third-party product that are specific to your product.

- The relationship between the third-party product vendor and your organization.
- The level of detail the audience needs in order to be successful.

Is the third-party product documentation available and accurate?

Evaluate the third-party documentation that exists for the product that your reader needs to interact with. Is this documentation readily available on the web? Is it up to date for the version of the product your reader needs to use? Does the documentation cover the content that your audience needs in order to complete the task? If the answers to these questions are all yes, your best option is to link directly to their documentation and say as little as possible in your own documentation. In this way, you reduce your maintenance cost to a single link.

If the answer to any of these questions is no, you might need to fall back to another option. Use the remaining factors to determine which one is the best fit.

Are there required settings or configurations in the third-party product that are specific to your product?

If third-party documentation exists but the coverage in that documentation is not enough for your audience to be successful with your own product or task, more coverage might be necessary. If there are specific settings, configurations, or decisions of any kind that your reader needs to handle in the third-party product in order for them to be successful with the integration or task, and those configurations are not obvious from the third-party documentation, you should document them. For example, consider a scenario where you are documenting a task for a software product that needs to receive data from a third-party product. For your product to be able to receive the data, the third-party product needs to be configured to produce it in a particular format. List the settings and values required to specify the format that your product expects, using the terminology of the third-party product, to ensure that your readers can be successful with overall goal. Do not phrase these parameters in the form of a procedure, and don't include screen shots if at all possible, as both can be rendered obsolete overnight. Instead, allow the third-party vendor documentation to handle any procedural detail, reference, or illustration. Your reference documentation covering only the specific parameters required for your use case should supplement their more comprehensive coverage of their product.

What is the relationship between the third-party product vendor and your organization?

If third-party documentation does not exist or is insufficient to cover the task that your audience will need to complete, resist the conclusion that you need to provide this documentation yourself. Instead, evaluate the relationship between your organization and the third-party product vendor. Perhaps your companies have a partnership or similar close relationship, which allows you to reach out to your counterparts in their organization. If they are writing their own documentation in concert with your efforts, the documentation you need might be available to your readers in time for your publication date. If you can collaborate and share your needs, both organizations benefit by designing docs that they are each able to maintain and by avoiding unnecessary duplication or conflicting information. Readers benefit when you consider the full scope of their needs.

In many situations, such collaboration is not possible. In that case, your way forward should depend on the previous factor: whether there are required settings or configurations in the third-party product that are specific to your product. If not, do not include any specific coverage of the third-party product and refer your customers to the third-party vendor for any questions. If there are, refer to the next question: the level of detail the audience needs to be successful.

What level of detail does your audience need in order to be successful?

Consider this question only if other factors have not led you to a conclusion that will allow your readers to be successful without unreasonably extending your support and maintenance burden beyond the scope of your own product. That is, if the third-party vendor does not offer documentation, your organization's relationship with the third-party vendor does not allow for collaboration, and specific settings or configurations in that third-party product are necessary for readers to be successful with the task you are documenting, you have two choices left. The option you choose should depend on the level of detail required by your audience. In order for the reader to be successful, does he or she need to be stepped through a detailed procedure in the third-party product, as opposed to more limited coverage of just those specific settings or configurations that need to be set?

As we stated before, if a detailed procedure *is not* required, provide limited coverage of the specific settings or parameters that your readers need to set in the third-party product. Do not phrase them as a procedure, and refer customers to the third-party vendor for any additional support needs.

If a detailed procedure *is* required, find a workaround that allows you to provide it outside of your formal documentation set. You might be able to contribute a post on your company blog or an article to a community site that covers the integrated procedure in detail, even including screenshots of that third-party product if necessary. In a less-formal, time-stamped location, your content helps your audience without incurring a support and maintenance cost to your organization. Link to this blog or community post

The Product is Docs

from the official product documentation, but keep the content separate.

When in doubt, use this decision tree

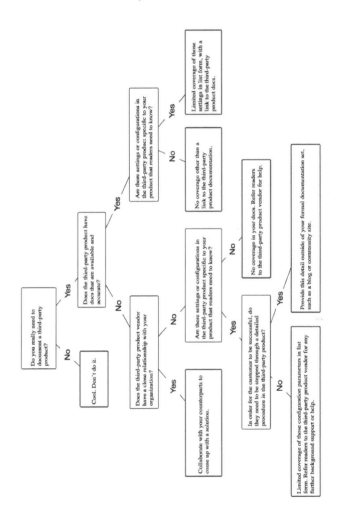

7. Hiring, Training, and Managing Documentation Teams

This chapter is unique in this book because it is the only one specifically written for managers of documentation teams and focused on some of the basic personnel activities that managers are responsible for. There hasn't been a lot written about this side of the profession, and the tech writing landscape has changed a lot in the last several years. How we hire, develop, and manage our teams is fundamental to our success.

Hiring tech writers for the 21st century

Technical writing is a career that you can transition into from a variety of professional and educational backgrounds. It is also a profession where someone can learn almost all the skills they need to be competent. So what makes a technical writer exceptional? Resourcefulness and eagerness are the key. When you screen tech writer candidates, look for a real appetite for discovery. The job, fundamentally, isn't about writing or learning technology. It's a relationship business, more like investigative journalism than anything else. Writers have to identify and cultivate your sources, they have to build mutual respect and trust, and they have to follow the story wherever it leads. Then they have to be able to organize that information and write about it clearly. But only then. In today's product development world, writers need to demonstrate that journalistic hunger.

Writers also have to be flexible, adaptable, and accepting of change. Schedules change, ideas evolve, product teams pivot. It is an adaptable, resourceful writer who is able to bend with these changes and produce relevant content. The technical background and product-related specifics are things that people can learn; the resourcefulness, the eagerness to learn, less so.

Good and consistent use of the English language is a must in a writing candidate, but mastery is not. Look for writers who can write clear sentences and organize information well, but someone who isn't afraid to break a rule or two when it serves to engage a modern reader. You do want someone who can internalize and adhere to a style guide, even if it requires them to write differently from the way they are accustomed to. They need to be able to adapt their writing to meet your standards and your audience requirements.

In terms of writing samples, good candidates will have taken the time to understand your company, have a rudimentary familiarity with its products and its market, and be able to show work and tell stories that demonstrate their ability to associate their previous work with the position they are applying for. Writing samples and portfolio carry a lot of weight, and it is also important in the interview to have the writer explain how he or she wrote the provided samples.

When we were discussing this chapter during its development, one of our managers also commented about the old stereotypes of what makes writers and developers different:

An idea persists that technical writers and developers are cut from different cloth. It suggests that the former would never understand the product but is good with language, and that the latter is terrible at communicating, but wonderfully competent with code. Each stereotype rolls their eyes at the other, certain they cannot possibly understand. Thus, one must hire a tech writer who understands and can work with the uncommunicative, deeply introverted engineers. That is irksome. At the first hint of this prejudice from a tech writing candidate, I am discouraged. Plenty of writers have a deep understanding of the product about which they write. Indeed, they are often the first end-users. And developers can be excellent communicators, progressively disclosing complex information naturally, because they have trained their peers or written dozens of blog posts to evangelize their product or idea. In today's documentation world, writers and developers use the same tools and the same project management methods. Let us move beyond the stereotypes and recognize that the boundary between writers and developers is thin and permeable.

At Splunk, we also look for writers who have a true passion for working directly with customers. Many companies have significant organizational barriers that prevent writers from talking directly with customers. Some writers are complacent about that, or even defeated. We look for candidates who find a way to engage directly with the community, even if there were obstacles to doing so.

If you are hiring writers for today's software world, you want writers who are:

- Flexible
- Fearless
- Personable
- Organized
- Experimental
- Customer-focused
- Generalists

Training tech writers in the 21st century

The principles of training and professional development for technical writers aren't much different from other product development teams. So, just a few comments here.

You want to secure a training budget, then use team training to create shared vocabulary and convey essential concepts and methods, such as topic-based information design and scenario-focused engineering. Individual writers will need specific training in different areas, whether through courses or direct mentoring. Consider which conferences are the right cultural and technical fit for your organization, and send writers to them regularly, as both attendees and presenters. Involve your department in meetups, not only for documentarians but for adjacent developer and devops interests as well. Determine what training your writers need to work hands-on with the products they document, and set goals for them to reach proficiency.

As with hiring, consider the balance of technical training and professional development that will emphasize creativity, experimentation, project management, and responsiveness to customer needs. Build capacity for these skills in your department, and they will serve you well in your information-development efforts as well as the broader collaborative picture within the product development group.

Managing documentation teams

As with training, the fundamentals of managing a documentation team are not unique. There are a few special considerations, though, that are worth your attention if you want to attune your management practices to focus on what matters most for writing technical documentation in a product development group.

Performance management in a cross-functional world

The fundamentals of performance management pertain to setting appropriate goals and measuring the results. It is a standard management principle that you see the behaviors (and results) that you measure for, so set goals that promote the same attributes you look for when you hire. It is easy for writers to focus on their feature work and subjugate themselves to the scrum process. And goals that prioritize on-time delivery, relevance, and accuracy are important. But you should also inspire their engagement and give them the autonomy to succeed. Manage doc team performance in a way that keeps writers focused on innovation, customer interaction, and collaboration. Set goals for these characteristics and reward writers who demonstrate them in tangible ways, so that they can serve as examples for the rest of the department and for the product development team as a whole.

See Chapter 10, "Measuring Success," for a related discussion.

Collective intelligence

Whatever your organizational structure, it remains true that the documentation team has the obligation to build a coherent, consistent information set for customers who want to use your products. The work of the documentation team spans multiple scrums and often represents the integration of technologies from multiple product teams. To help each other—and the customers— succeed, writers need to watch and listen at all times for information that might be relevant to another writing colleague. It goes beyond sharing information. It requires informed, lateral thinking and a clear understanding of the overall product context. Whether you call this "shared consciousness," "joint cognition," or (as we do in the Splunk doc team) "collective intelligence," you have to instill this practice in the cultural fabric of your department. Unless your company is very sophisticated about portfolio management, or is successfully practicing scenario-focused engineering across scrum teams and product lines, the burden of achieving collective intelligence will fall on the writers.

Team size and types of information deliverables

The size of your team can also play a role in the types of documentation that you choose to provide.

When the company is very small, your writer or writers will likely provide all the written product material for the company. Writers will work with Agile teams to document product functionality and usage instructions, as well as marketing datasheets, technical whitepapers, support knowledge base articles, and even slide decks for the sales team to use.

As the organization and the documentation team grows to a medium size, the company is likely to have developed more specialized teams to create different types of product information. The organization will also have a larger engineering team and more regular product releases. As pressure mounts on the documentation team to deliver complete product documentation for each release, the documentation team might choose to focus exclusively on product usage documentation to satisfy the essential requirements with its available staff. Other specialized teams might take on the work of writing marketing materials, white papers, support articles, and sales support materials.

As the organization and the documentation team grows yet larger, the documentation team might regain the size and flexibility to begin delivering documentation that goes beyond strict feature information and usage instructions. This is a time to begin providing end-to-end user scenarios that span multiple features and possibly multiple products. You might start to join forces with the other specialized groups in the company that provide product-related information, such as the training and education services group and the marketing or technical marketing groups. At Splunk, we use the concept of Integrated Content Experience to describe this type of collaboration, where we use a set of governing scenarios that span marketing, technical documentation, and customer education to shape a meaningful information journey for customers.

Team growth and shrinkage

Any organization that writes documentation in a product development organization is likely to exist in a very dynamic environment. Companies, departments, and individual teams will rarely be static for long. As the needs of the organization change, your documentation team might experience periods of growth—adding new team members—and periods of shrinkage—reductions in team size—over time.

Team size, and the dynamics of growth and reduction, present additional factors to consider when deciding how to best create documentation in a product development environment.

Challenges of a growing team

Using ratios to plan growth
Typically, if your company is growing, the doc team will grow with it. As specific projects and programs get funded, writer positions should open accordingly. In many cases, upper-level engineering management will be interested to use a ratio of writers to developers to allocate resources. The optimal ratio of developers to writer is mythical and not that useful, but it is persistent. If you, as a doc team manager, are involved in conversations about the ratio, be sure to make a couple of points:

• The ratio should not focus on developers, because developers are not the only people who create work for technical writers. The ratio should consider all the people who make work for technical writers, including developers, designers, product managers, testers, and customer support engineers.

• The answer depends on what the developers are doing. You can assign a team of eight developers to spend six months working on performance, and their dedicated effort will result in just a few days of documentation work. On the other hand, two UI developers working for a week could keep a team of several tech writers busy for a month.

To arrive at an intelligent ratio, you need to include an accurate number of constituents and weight the developer number itself based on the type of work they are doing. With these two considerations, you might arrive at a number for your company that can guide resource planning.

A corollary ratio of number of scrum teams per writer is also worth introducing to the conversation. No matter how good the writer-to-others ratio looks, if there are too many scrum teams, writers will not be able to work efficiently or effectively because they will have too many contexts to cover.

Managing complexity

With growth, you get complexity. Communication becomes more complex at all levels: among individual contributors, within and across teams, among multiple parallel product development projects. No one person can track all product development activities in significant detail. Writers on a larger team might specialize in particular areas of the product, which can lead to knowledge silos and lack of redundant coverage. The drive to cultivate versatile generalists will suffer under the pressures of acquiring deep knowledge about specific technologies.

A larger team working in a more complex product environment also leads to greater opportunities (and responsibilities) for doc team members to independently manage their work and highlight issues that might affect other team members. Here we come back to the idea of collective intelligence. It is significantly harder to achieve, and significantly more important, in a larger team.

Larger organizations need more process. Focus on developing light processes that will reduce the time writers spend trying to figure out *how* to do their work, so they can spend more time actually doing it. Processes such as these should also enable you to build an effective, repeatable training experience for new team members, so that writers who are joining your team don't create extra work for existing team members.

Another tool to help manage complexity is the development of standards. A well-developed style guide and glossary, along with peer reviews or formal editing, will ensure consistent terminology and usage. If you are working in a structured authoring environment, the development of topic types and standardized information architecture will also reduce some of the unnecessary variation that comes with complexity.

Finally, if your team is growing rapidly, you need to consider how to retain the camaraderie of a small team while adding new members and adapting to cultural change across the organization. Hire carefully, define and announce the culture to new hires from day one, and use the key aspects of your culture to inform goal-setting and performance management.

Challenges of a shrinking team

Growth and shrinkage are cyclical, so you and your department will likely face both. If your company is experiencing lean times, you need to take care of your remaining employees and help them stay focused on their essential tasks.

If your team is getting smaller, ratios might be part of the conversation (see "Using ratios to plan growth," above).

Rigorously prioritize what the team works on. Use customer feedback and learning objectives to ensure that you are focusing on what is relevant and useful for customers. Engage with leadership to promote the importance of a positive user experience and good documentation in ensuring customer satisfaction. Don't let this work get lost in the mix of fewer people doing more work, and possibly a drive to reduce costs. In a shrinking team, you literally can't afford to do anything else.

As a team gets smaller, people need to cover areas previously covered by a specialized writer. Cross-functional teams are also undergoing similar changes as they shrink. It is important to capture and maintain whatever knowledge you can when a team is larger, and essential to do so—and use what you have captured— when a team is getting smaller.

If a doc team is shrinking due to reduced development of new features for a mature product, focus on how you can streamline the existing content, improve the user experience, and further reduce ongoing support costs.

If a doc team is shrinking due to higher growth in another area of the company, actively connect team members with those new opportunities. The individuals and the company will benefit, both in the short term and the long.

Conclusion

If you can, scale your documentation team, no matter its size, to support a direct participation model. If you are in a situation in which a proportionally very small team needs to support a proportionally very large development organization and each writer would have to cover five or more scrum teams, consider adopting the scrum of writers approach and be very specific about the kinds of deliverables that the documentation team will provide.

Be prepared to evaluate the best option for you at any phase of your growth, and be prepared to adapt based on your current situation and on where you see future trends of growth or shrinkage for your organization and team. Just as you want to cultivate flexibility in your writers, cultivate it in yourself as a manager as well.

8. Learning Objectives

Learning objectives come to us from instructional design. At Splunk, we have found it useful to apply learning objectives as a planning tool for documentation. In combination with our audience definitions (see Chapter 3, "Audience"), learning objectives enable us to envision and plan content that aligns with specific customer needs and solves a tangible problem.

What is a learning objective?

A learning objective is an intended intellectual goal or outcome. Learning objectives are relevant to many instructional contexts. In technical documentation, learning objectives provide direction and structure for writers planning content. They also set expectations for users.

You can categorize learning objectives broadly into a few types.

- Awareness
  - o The user should be able to describe or paraphrase a concept or feature, or summarize a list of options.
  - o Example: Identify the available alert types and triggering options.
- Comprehension
  - o Depending on the type of content in the topic, the user should be able to make a decision about how the concept or feature applies to their use case. The user could explain pros and cons of the options presented in the topic.
  - o Example: Apply an alert type and triggering option to a specific scenario.
- Applicable skill
  - o The user should be able to follow instructions to complete a task successfully.
  - o Example: Set up a scheduled alert.

Note: this is a simpler scheme than the one proposed in Julie Dirksen's *Design for How People Learn* (p. 69)[2]. This scheme is based on our own direct experience, and hers offers a useful comparison.

Learning objective vs. user goal

The authors of *Developing Quality Technical Information* (*DQTI*) emphasize the importance of focusing on users' goals and identifying tasks that support these goals (pp. 32-8).

When you write, apply user goals to define an over-arching purpose for topics, chapters, and manuals. Identifying user goals can be a helpful first step in discovering and establishing learning objectives.

Learning objectives are distinct from user goals, although they are strongly connected. User goals are pragmatic or real-world goals; usually, they involve finding a solution to a problem, making a decision, or completing a task. Learning objectives are intellectual in nature; they support user goals by identifying the awareness, comprehension, or skills that a user needs to meet a real-world goal.

Here is an illustration of how user goals and learning objectives relate.

User goal

What real-world goal or outcome is the user trying to achieve?

- Example goal: Monitor login failures in real time.

Learning objectives

What does the user need to know to achieve this goal? How much does the user need to know? How would a user demonstrate their knowledge?

Here are some example objectives to support the goal above. Note that, while objectives are not user goals, they indicate

---

[2] *Design for How People Learn*, Second Edition, Julie Dirksen, New Riders, 2015.

intellectual tasks (such as identifying, explaining, distinguishing between options, deciding, following steps) that a user can perform in a real-world scenario.

- Example objectives:
  - The user should be able to identify and explain to a coworker the available alert types and triggering options.
  - The user should be able to choose an alert type and triggering option for a specific use case.
  - The user should be able to follow and, depending on the procedure's complexity, independently repeat the steps to create a real-time alert with per-result triggering. The user should be able to describe the alert configurations and the behavior that result from this task.

These learning objectives, once met, support a user goal of monitoring login failures. Once the user can identify alerting options, choose which alert type and triggering options to apply to their scenario, and can create that alerting behavior that they need successfully, the user is able to monitor login failures.

Users (and writers) as learners

Writers can benefit from thinking of users not just as readers, but learners. Technical writers do not document a product for the sake of enumerating all of its parts or features; rather, writers craft documentation to support user learning and success. As the principles of minimalism tell us, our customers are reading either to *learn* or to *do*. Learning objectives provide the bridge to address both cases.

Documentation audiences typically represent many experience or comfort levels with a product or feature. It is important to consider where you might need to meet users in a given topic.

Thinking of your users as learners can help you focus your own research efforts. Put yourself into a user's shoes as often as possible. Your questions and discovery process might mirror many aspects of a user's experience.

If you are thinking of users as learners, you might think of yourself as an instructor. This is partly true, but it is useful to remember that writers are learners too. Writers aren't necessarily subject matter experts on a particular feature or product, at least not at the outset of a documentation project. A writer must also start as a learner.

Staying in both an instructor's and a learner's frame of mind can be immensely beneficial for a writer. Your own learning experience might resemble that of a typical user. Your questions or points of confusion might give you insight into the kinds of things a user might also want to know or struggle with. As a writer, you are positioned to use your own learning experience to influence your documentation work.

Curiosity is one of a technical writer's most valuable tools or qualities. Being curious and asking questions never hurts, of course, but remember that, when doing research, you might sometimes learn more than a user needs to know. Depending on your audience, users might also need information presented in a different order, format, or style from those in which you gathered it. Holding onto an instructor's frame of mind helps you sift and sort your own research findings for the essential points to cover. It also helps you find effective ways to present them in terms that will match the expectations and mental models of your customers.

Another benefit to seeing users as learners is that it boosts your empathy for users and their goals. We've all had a variety of learning experiences and we've all probably faced challenging concepts or confusing instructions as part of trying to achieve one goal or another. As you transform your discoveries into documentation, you can aim to facilitate the impactful and friendly learning experiences that any learner appreciates. Empathizing with users as learners also helps when handling feedback.

For more information, see Chapter 11, "Research for Technical Writers."

Charting a course

A learning objective is like a marker on a map. A learning objective's exit criteria, such as being able to identify available configurations or follow a task successfully, indicate where a user should be by the time they finish reading or using a topic. For the technical writer, the objective indicates an intended destination and informs content planning, research, and creation. Writers must chart the most efficient and effective course from a starting point to that destination.

Starting points and destinations

Charting a course to a destination on a map or in documentation only works if you establish your starting point clearly (Dirksen, 63). This is essential for both the user and the writer.

For a writer, being able to indicate the starting point depends on knowing your audience and understanding the goals that users in that audience are most likely trying to accomplish when they land on your topic (see Mark Baker's discussion of "information foraging" in *Every Page is Page One*)[3].

A clearly-defined starting point can help users decide quickly whether a topic is going to serve their needs. It also helps a user understand how a specific topic fits into a broader documentation set and how to navigate that documentation set.

Writers can establish the user's starting position at the beginning of a topic. Present enough context to orient users before they delve into the main content. As part of acknowledging the audience and goals that your topic supports, it might be necessary to establish prerequisites for a topic or task. A brief introductory paragraph can also help the user understand if a topic fits their use case or if they need to find a different topic.

---

[3] *Every Page is Page One*, Mark Baker, XML Press, 2013, p. 3.

The starting point to destination balance: One to one? Many to one?

A technical writer might need to write a particular topic for an audience with varied experience levels, but this does not impact or change the starting point for a given objective.

It is important to be aware of the various places a user might or might not have been prior to arriving at one's topic and the different levels of experience that a topic's audience comprises. But a given topic must be able to stand alone. This is not to say that a topic might not need to "establish context" (Baker, 78) or address situational differences (deployments, configurations, cautions, and the like) that users encounter over the course of moving from start to destination. But addressing these differences must still serve the topic's learning objective.

In *Every Page is Page One*, Mark Baker offers a helpful set of principal characteristics of Every Page is Page One-style topics (Baker 78).

- Self-contained
- Specific and limited purpose
- Establish context
- Assume the reader is qualified
- Stay on one level of detail

These characteristics are helpful for checking whether a given topic has a clear enough starting point and destination.

Route vs. scenery

Getting users from point A to point B efficiently requires a distinct focus on the topic's learning objective. The content that ends up in a topic is as much a product of a writer figuring out what belongs in the topic as it is a reflection of figuring out what does not belong in that topic.

Plan topic scope carefully. It is helpful to remember that no one topic can cover every possible scenario and all of the available "backstory" on a feature or product. Trying to do so often results in duplicate content and heightens the risk of inaccuracy and/or maintenance headaches. It can also introduce content that just does not support your audience's user goals and instead distracts or complicates.

Not every topic has the same kind of learning objective. Depending on a topic's learning objective and the kind of topic you are writing, it might be necessary to keep a user's focus tightly on a relatively narrow route. Let other topics fill in the context or describe additional options. For example, a task topic should assume that a user is already equipped with prerequisite information. Steps in the task do not need to include notes or supplemental details beyond what is necessary to complete them. Before introducing the task, include prerequisites to help users ensure that they are ready to follow the steps.

There might be other topics in which it is appropriate to call the user's attention thoughtfully to the occasional bit of scenery. If a topic's objective is to help a user identify different configuration options or equip a user to make a decision between options for different scenarios, it might be helpful to include contextual information, best practices, or other information that supports this objective.

Topic as vehicle

To extend this already perhaps too-elaborate analogy of objective-as-destination, let's consider the documentation topic as vehicle or conveyance for getting users from point A to point B. Although it might seem merely an amusing exercise, it is actually quite helpful for writers to consider the mechanical aspects of a topic, chapter, and/or manual. In particular, this consideration can help you with maintaining existing content.

Whether you are writing new content or reviewing existing material, use this analogy to assist you in considering whether a topic is as sound and functional as it should be. In so doing, take your scrutiny to the level of sentences, phrases, and words. Do your word choice, phrasing, and sentence structure serve the learning objective? If not, there is likely a better and clearer approach to consider. Eliminate unnecessary words, explanations, and any content that does not have some role, like part of an efficient machine, in delivering the user from point A to point B over the course of the topic.

Writers can benefit tremendously from regarding the topic as machine. This is not to say that topics cannot have a friendly, human, tone. Rather, the suggestion is to streamline content; invest in the leanest set of solid, efficient, parts you can find instead of constructing an overly elaborate, possibly distracting, structure. Be your own mechanic or engineer as you write. Tinker and cut ruthlessly in service of the learning objective.

For more details on maintaining content, see Chapter 9, "Maintaining Existing Content."

Topics and objectives

Every topic needs a learning objective

Every topic should have a learning objective. You might even say that every paragraph in a topic needs an objective or sub-objective.

Why learning objectives are a topic's best friend

Easier to research and write

- Topics with learning objectives have a well-defined audience and, in turn, support specific user goals. They are user-oriented, helping customers solve real-world problems. They do not merely document the product for the sake of documenting the product.
- A topic without a learning objective has no particular direction. It is difficult to know how to approach the topic in the first place. What information belongs in it? Who is it

for? Lacking a learning objective, a writer is less likely to be able to do effective research with engineers or other SMEs.

Easier to organize

- Topics with learning objectives are easier to organize, because the flow of sections and paragraphs is oriented logically towards a user goal and the objectives that equip the user to get there. A user goal helps you lay out the story your topic tells.
- Lacking an objective, it is very hard to structure a topic. In what order should the content go? Are there any prerequisites? Where do you begin? How can you tell when to conclude? The most essential information can be scattered throughout a topic, buried in the midst of less relevant or goal-oriented content.

Easier to maintain

- Topics with learning objectives, because they have a clear and logical structure, are easier to maintain. Learning objectives give you a bigger picture to work with and against which you can evaluate the impact of feature or product updates. A topic with learning objectives makes it easier to decide where to make changes.
- Topics without learning objectives can feel like a hodgepodge or random collection of points. As features or a product evolve, it can be difficult to determine what gaps might exist and how to address them because it's not clear what *should* be in the topic to begin with. They can also overlap or duplicate content in other topics that *do* have clear learning objectives. This is no help to users or writers.
- Topics without learning objectives can also be harder to maintain from one version to another. Without a clear sense of what goals or objectives the topic aims to support or what audience the topic serves, it can be hard to determine the impact from feature updates.

Easier to use
- Topics with learning objectives set clear user expectations. Users can decide quickly whether a topic fits their use case or experience level and, if the topic does suit their needs, they are more likely to find the content helpful. Well-defined learning objectives help you get users from point A to point B without missing important information, overwhelming users with extra details, or sending users on an unexpected detour.
- Topics written without a learning objective are more likely to frustrate readers. These topics don't set clear expectations, and users don't necessarily know if they are in a good starting place from which to use the content. It can be hard to navigate a topic without a learning objective. Imagine/recall the frustration of attending a lecture or day of class when an instructor has not considered a learning objective and the content, activities, or time management that would support it.

Can a topic have more than one learning objective?

Generally, it seems best to have one learning objective for a topic. This rule of thumb helps you create more modular content and reduces the chance of writing content that overlaps with the work of other writers. If a topic serves one learning objective, it is much easier to determine what content belongs in it and what content does not. It is also easier to keep users oriented to one learning objective in a given topic rather than trying to address many needs all at once.

It might, however, sometimes be less practical to separate content into different topics for different learning objectives. In such cases, if learning objectives are closely related, it's best to include all of the content in one topic. Focus on optimizing for a straightforward, easily navigable, documentation user experience.

Using learning objectives separately and together

Several learning objectives might combine to support one user goal. A user might progress through multiple topics, each with a different kind of learning objective (awareness, comprehension, applicable skill) as they move towards a particular user goal.

Learning objectives should be modular; like building blocks, you should be able to use them together or separately. Each block can also (potentially) be reused to support a different goal. To illustrate this idea, let's go back to the example goal and objectives above and consider a different scenario.

Two users might work together to solve the real-world problem of monitoring login failures in real time. The first user's goal might be to research available alerting options, decide which one best fits the situation, and explain their choice to another user. The other user's goal might be to set up the selected alert. Thus, the first user's goal is met by awareness and comprehension objectives, while the second user's goal is met by an applicable skill learning objective. The first user does not necessarily need to know how to create an alert. This user doesn't necessarily need to know about other alerting options.

Modular learning objectives help you meet users where they are and get them to a specific kind of proficiency. As the example scenario shows, they can also help you to follow a progressive disclosure model in your content.

To help you create more modular learning objectives, you can use a tool like a Learning Objective Matrix to identify the audience that you are targeting and the specific kind of awareness, comprehension, or applicable skill that this audience needs. The matrix can help you pinpoint comfort or experience levels and specific exit criteria. Here is an example:

LEARNING OBJECTIVE MATRIX

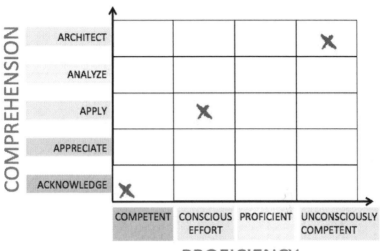

On the Y axis, levels measure how you want your readers to be able to use the content you're presenting to them. The bottom is the lowest level of comprehension; the top is the highest, or deepest level of comprehension. The position of a learning objective in the matrix indicates the quantity and quality of documentation necessary for a reader to achieve the objective.

- **Acknowledge** = a level of comprehension where a user can say, "I know feature X exists and, at a high level, what it does."
- **Appreciate** = "I know what feature X can do for me" or "how I can leverage this feature with other things to have better success with my use case."
- **Apply** = "Get this set up, installed, launched, configured, running."
- **Analyze** = "I have set up my new system, and now I am figuring out how to improve efficiency, performance, or results."
- **Architect** = "I can design and create my own artifact."

On the X axis are the degrees to which you want your learners to be proficient with what they have learned. The left is the lowest level of proficiency; the right is the most competent you can get.

- **Competent** = the point at which a user can say, "I'll follow the directions word for word and do this once, perhaps never again."
- **Conscious effort** = the point at which a user can say, "If this is an open-book exam, I'm cool, I can use the feature/product."
- **Proficient** = the point at which a user can say, "Don't need the instructions any more. I can totally do what I'm supposed to without any trouble."
- **Unconsciously competent** = "I am the master, I can even teach others."

How do you use this Learning Objective Matrix?

- Plot on the matrix. Start by imagining something you want the user to be able to do after having read your documentation, and attempt to position it on the matrix.
- Write the learning objective. Use a learning objective template. Be meticulous in the verbs you use to reflect the level of proficiency and comprehension. Avoid general words like "Understand." Pick a verb, then construct a learning objective, user-story style: "After having read the documentation, I want to be able to paraphrase what stacked charts do and how I can benefit from using them."
- Adjust plotting. Validate that you have accurately plotted the learning objective on the matrix. In practice, it's useful to write the learning objectives on the matrix.
- Repeat. Write up a bunch of learning objectives for the feature. For input, use your own brainstorming, and any relevant input from a product manager or engineer.
- Share and discuss. With a list of plotted-out learning objectives, you can now discuss with your scrum team to get some feedback into your expected deliverables.

Sharing the matrix helps to frame the discussion with the product manager and other stakeholders so that everyone has a clearer picture of what the documentation will be, and what it will do for the customer.

This tool frees you from operating within the mindset of an outline, or thinking about how to structure the content too early. At this point, the focus is squarely on the user and what they need, not on how you're going to present the information.

Meta-objectives and sub-objectives

While it is often best to have one learning objective for each topic, there are often "meta" and "sub" objectives for each topic. These can be helpful for writers planning how to organize a topic. Consider how a particular topic and its objective serve a larger intellectual purpose for the user. Consider also how that same topic might require the user to meet several sub- or mini learning objectives in order to achieve the main one. No single topic can address the meta-objective by itself. It is also not practical or appropriate to try to have different topics address the sub-objectives separately.

For example, an overview topic on different alert types and triggering options might have user awareness of these types and options as its objective. The meta-objective in this case is user comprehension of alerting capability in the product. An example sub-objective might be user awareness of real-time alert triggering options.

Writing with learning objectives in mind

Who makes learning objectives?

You do. A writer should identify and specify learning objectives for a topic or set of topics. That being said, learning objectives do not originate in a vacuum. Learning objectives are not usually spelled out in feature development artifacts like requirements documentation or product specs, but they have roots in the earliest phases of the development cycle. They are often impacted by changes and decisions made over the course of feature development. For this reason, it's important for writers to be aware of feature development work in their scrums and to participate in team discussions throughout the process.

What does a strong learning objective look like?

Going back to our earlier analogy, a good learning objective is like a clear marker on a map. It tells you where you should be at the end of a set of directions.

Julie Dirksen suggests that a learning objective needs to be action-oriented (Dirksen, 65). She writes:

When you are creating learning objectives, ask yourself:

- Is this something the learner would actually do in the real world?
- Can I tell when they've done it?

If your answer to either of these questions is no, then you might want to reconsider your learning objective.

Dirksen's advice is helpful here. It recalls important principles discussed in this chapter. To build on her suggestions, here is a list of qualities to consider when assessing a learning objective.

- Does the learning objective reflect a strong audience definition?
- Is the learning objective appropriate for the audience experience level?
- Does the objective support a real-world user goal?
- Is the objective rooted in a clear starting point?
- Does the objective indicate a clear destination?
  - Does the objective have well-defined exit criteria? Will the user be better equipped to solve a problem, create something, or make a decision after reading this topic?
- Can the objective be categorized into one of the following types?

- o Awareness
  - The user should be able to describe or paraphrase a concept or feature, or summarize a list of options.
- o Comprehension
  - Depending on the type of content in the topic, the user should be able to make a decision about how the concept or feature applies to their use case. The user could explain pros and cons of the options presented in the topic.
- o Applicable skill
  - The user should be able to follow instructions to complete a task successfully.

Here is an example. This objective might not require an entire topic of its own.

User goal:
Customize a data visualization to show a daily sales total in different colors depending on whether it is above or below a certain level.

Learning objective:
The user should be able to follow and repeat the steps to configure the visualization in the product's user interface.

Criteria for a strong learning objective	How the objective meets this criterion
Does the objective support a real-world user goal?	The user should be able to follow configuration steps, resulting in a customized visualization.
Is the user better equipped to solve a problem, create	

Criteria for a strong learning objective	How the objective meets this criterion
something, or make a decision after reading this topic?	
Is the objective rooted in a clear starting point?	Before meeting this objective, users should be familiar with the given data visualization type and be able to select it to represent data in a specific use case. They should also be able to describe the available configuration options for the visualization.
Does the objective indicate a clear destination?	By achieving this learning objective, users are equipped to configure the visualization. Depending on the complexity of the steps, users might be able to independently repeat the steps or describe the steps to another user.
Can the objective be categorized into one of the following types? • Awareness • Comprehension • Applicable skill	Applicable skill

How to tell when a learning objective needs to be refined

Sometimes a learning objective needs to be refined or broken down into separate objectives. It might be too vague or broad. Dirksen suggests that if it doesn't indicate something a user could do in the real world or you wouldn't be able to tell if a user has done it, then a learning objective isn't clear enough.

Having a learning objective in the first place is better than not having a learning objective at all. From here, you can refine the objective so that it helps you generate effective content or clean up existing content. The most common problem for learning objectives is over-reaching. Trying to accomplish too much is problematic in a few ways. Primarily, it defeats a topic's ability to make effective use of the user's time and attention. It also defeats the topic's ability to fit into a cohesive and navigable documentation unit (topic set, chapter, manual). It causes issues for other topics, making their boundaries vague or weakening their connection to learning objectives. When you encounter an over-reaching learning objective, break it into separate objectives.

The other problematic kind of learning objective involves trying to help users work around poor design. Supporting an unclear UI or a confusing workflow results in vague or non-modular learning objectives. This kind of learning objective usually can't be refined into something stronger. It's better to go back to your scrum team to talk about ways to improve the feature for a better user experience. This is another reason why considering learning objectives early and often in the development cycle is a valuable practice.

Here is an example of a problematic learning objective. Note that the user goal is not, in itself, problematic.

User goal

Customize a data visualization to show a daily sales total in different colors depending on whether it is above or below a certain level.

Learning objective (before refining)
Understand the available visualization options, choose the right visualization for the use case, learn what configurations are available for the visualization, and make configurations in the user interface.

Assessment
Recall our learning objective criteria:

Criteria for a strong learning objective	How the objective meets this criterion
Does the objective support a real-world user goal? Is the user better equipped to solve a problem, create something, or make a decision after reading this topic?	The user should be able to follow configuration steps, resulting in a customized visualization.
Is the objective rooted in a clear starting point?	Before meeting this objective, users should be familiar with the given data visualization type and be able to select it to represent data in a specific use case. They should also be able to describe the available configuration options for the visualization.
Does the objective indicate a clear destination?	By achieving this learning objective, users are equipped to configure the visualization. Depending on the

Criteria for a strong learning objective	How the objective meets this criterion
	complexity of the steps, users might be able to independently repeat the steps or describe the steps to another user.
Can the objective be categorized into one of the following types? • Awareness • Comprehension • Applicable skill	Applicable skill

As it stands, this learning objective needs to be refined.

Refining the objective

To start, this objective does not support the user goal. It is vague and seems to encompass too many different objectives Let's go back to some initial questions for defining a learning objective:

What does the user need to know to achieve this goal? How much does the user need to know? How would a user know that they have met the learning objective?

There are actually just a few things that a user should know specifically in order to make customizations.

• What configuration tool is available in the UI.
• What settings are available in the tool.
• How to make configurations using the tool.

Next, let's reconsider a starting point. Given what we've established about what the user needs to know specifically to accomplish the goal, we can rule out other things that the user should already understand.

- The user should already be able to describe the available visualization options.
- The user should already be able to select the visualization that fits their use case.
- The user should also already be able to describe what components are configurable in this particular visualization.

This helps us reorient the objective. We can focus on users who are clear on all of the above but who need to know how to follow and repeat steps for configuring the visualization.

Let's refine the destination now and focus on a specific exit criterion. Isolate exactly where the user will end up when they achieve this objective:

> The user should be able to follow and repeat the steps to configure the visualization in the product's user interface.

At this point, it's clearer that the type of objective we need to define is mainly an applicable skill.

Refined objective

Follow and repeat the provided steps to configure the data visualization. The user should also be able to describe the effect of the configurations that they made.

After refining the objective, we've established a clearer starting point and destination. It is also much clearer what belongs in the topic or content section that supports this objective and what does not belong. Creating and organizing this content is now simpler. Maintaining it as updates occur is also more straightforward. In addition, the clearer starting point and destination mean that users can more easily recognize whether this content meets their needs.

Resources for generating learning objectives

For new features, a writer must often create a set of documentation topics. For updates to features, the writer is more likely to produce a single topic or updates to one or more topics. In any case, every piece of new content and every (considered) edit to existing content should be informed by a learning objective. The resources available to a given writer will vary depending on the team and company structure, but here are some suggestions that you might find helpful.

Cross-functional team

It can be helpful for product managers to draft the user goals for a feature or product. Talk to your team's product manager about user goals and look for information in product specs or requirements documentation.

If you have learning objectives in mind after gathering initial details about user goals, you can run the objectives by the product manager and developers on your team to get feedback. Learning objectives should fit into the team's overall vision for how users will use a particular feature. Keep the communication lines open as you work on your documentation.

Sales and support engineers can be a good source of audience information. These engineers typically work directly with users and can relay important feedback, frustrations, or other aspects of the audience for a particular feature or product. Use this information to shape learning objectives.

To get help with content or information architecture, talk to your documentation colleagues. Ask them about the learning objectives and content you are planning. When you have documentation ready to review, see if your colleagues' user experience matches your expected outcomes for external users.

Product specs

Read product requirements and specifications to understand user stories and the intended effects, benefits, or other outcomes of a feature development. Take a look at use cases that a product manager identifies. These will help you identify your audience to some degree and to understand the user goals intended for the feature. Remember that user goals are not exactly the same as learning objectives. If requirements and specs are not available or do not address user stories and use cases, ask questions and encourage your scrum team to provide these.

Engineering internal documentation

Internal engineering docs can be helpful for considering more constrained objectives, such as making users aware of particular configuration settings or permissions. More generally, while product specs are useful for identifying broader learning objectives, engineering internal docs can help you figure out how to get the user there. This kind of documentation can contain more information than users need, so consider carefully what to include and what to exclude or treat lightly in user documentation. Remember that creating relevant content is more important than creating comprehensive content.

User experience or design documents

Design documents and discussions also have important influence on learning objectives. Understanding how users might work with a feature and the questions or issues they might encounter is a key part of planning documentation that educates and empowers users. It is also important to advocate for the best possible user experience in the product. Advocating for users and asking questions from start to finish helps a writer generate documentation whose objectives are easier to define and support. It also helps writers avoid creating documentation that has as its objective being an aid or workaround to a difficult user interface or workflow.

Quality assurance

Quality assurance test plans or notes from testing can help you anticipate user experience and learning needs. For example, testing can uncover unexpected aspects of a workflow or feature functionality.

User feedback

User feedback can be helpful for showing you whether a topic is identifying and supporting a learning objective effectively. For example, if users consistently offer feedback that they are looking for content that a particular topic does not include, it might mean that the topic does not establish its objective clearly at the beginning. You might need to orient users more clearly to the topic's starting point and destination. Additionally, if users are confused by some part of the content or are asking clarifying questions on a regular basis, it might mean that the content is not supporting the established learning objective strongly enough.

The fact that users take the time to provide feedback, positive or negative, reminds us that reading and following documentation— in other words, learning—requires time and effort. Some of this is unavoidable, but strong learning objectives and strongly supportive content create effective and efficient learning experiences for your users.

Conclusion

This has been a brief tour of learning objectives and what technical writers can do with them. While this chapter offers our own perspective and discoveries, we encourage readers to explore the many available books and online resources devoted to learning objectives.

You can use the advice and information here to help you drive many technical writing goals. Some of the additional areas where learning objectives can be useful include the following.

- Defining audience
- Maintaining existing content
- Working with engineers
- Information architecture
- Testing documentation for accuracy
- Handling user feedback

These aspects are covered in other chapters of this book.

Working with learning objectives is a great way to connect with your users. It helps you create a documentation user experience that educates and empowers.

9. Maintaining Existing Content

> "...from so simple a beginning endless forms most beautiful and most wonderful have been, and are being, evolved." Charles Darwin, *On the Origin of Species,* 1859.

Evolution, both in a product and in its documentation, is something for writers to embrace and to initiate. Documentation maintenance lets writers create reliable content that evolves to meet user needs over time.

Build trust with your users by keeping content maintenance for supported software versions on your to-do list. Keeping existing content accurate, user-friendly, and fresh helps you to maintain user experience integrity and quality. No matter how long it has been around, every "page" or topic in a documentation set represents an opportunity to make a positive first impression on your users.

When does content need maintenance?

Maintenance is both a reactive and a proactive task. Writers can embark on documentation maintenance projects in response to feature updates or outside of development work.

Existing feature evolution

While writers spend time following new feature development and in response add new documentation content, existing software continues to evolve. Documentation must stay in step with this evolution. This type of update is usually spurred by development or sustaining work from engineering. User feedback and requests, other software dependencies, product enhancements, or bug fixes can prompt a team to change existing functionality.

The scope of feature evolution can help you to determine the scope of maintenance updates. If a single configuration setting changes, for example, maintenance updates are often fairly discrete. You might update the setting name and description, as well as any examples, in a single topic. If functionality changes are broader, they often warrant a more extensive update to the docs. Users need new guidance on how the updated product or feature works and there are often new use cases or scenarios to incorporate into the documentation. This kind of update is closer to new content development. It involves more conceptual reorientation, requiring a writer to reconsider product user experience, intended audience, and other factors.

Documentation evolution outside of feature updates

Even when the features or functionality that you document do not change, you might still need or want to make maintenance updates. There are several scenarios in which a writer might identify a need for content updates outside of feature development.

User feedback

User feedback is essential to maintaining existing content. Users might point out anything from a simple typo to larger errors. They can also provide more general feedback about a topic's structure or content.

New features or products from other teams or scrums

Changes beyond the features that you document might necessitate a mention, clarification, or other updates in your content. For example, users might gain the option to use your company's software in the cloud in addition to using on-premises installations. Depending on the documentation team's approach to such changes, content might need to become more agnostic or inclusive regarding customer deployment type. You might need to adjust content to serve more customers and/or a wider variety of deployment types.

New features that bear some relationship to your material can require you to rethink your content. Perhaps, for example, the new feature provides a better way to accomplish a similar goal under some circumstances. Your existing material then needs updating to reference that new feature and provide guidance on how to determine which feature to employ, based on the user's need.

User or audience considerations and evolution

A changing customer base can mean that the audience for a feature and its documentation starts to represent different experience levels, primary languages, or business roles. Considering and reconsidering audience can help you identify topics or other content that need to evolve in order to meet users where they are.

Not all users who are new to your company's software are using the latest version. Use regular docs maintenance to make a strong first impression on any user who lands on any currently supported version's documentation.

The material might not align with the current emphasis on particular use cases. Perhaps the company is now focusing on a somewhat different audience with different needs since the feature was developed. It can also happen that, once customers start using a feature, they use it in ways that were not anticipated when you first documented it.

Learning objective assessments

Assessing how, how well, or whether a topic supports learning objectives is closely connected to considering the audience for a topic and how that audience's needs or expectations might have evolved over time. Learning objectives can be a great help when you are evaluating content for revision. Ensuring that a topic represents and supports well-defined learning objectives is essential to setting and meeting user expectations in existing content. See Chapter 8, "Learning Objectives," for more details on this approach to content creation and maintenance.

New style guidelines

Style guidelines can evolve independently of the product. The audience for your documentation might change and new approaches to style or tone can develop in turn. One example is that a growing company will have an increasingly international customer base, and you might need to update existing content for a global audience. Standards in the wider software or documentation world also change and your content might need to adapt accordingly. Documentation editors can provide style guidance. Follow available internal guidelines and consult approved secondary sources to check whether your content needs updating.

New terminology

Without the product changing, names for and within the product can evolve. Writers should stay tuned for updates on product terminology from product managers, legal and marketing departments, or from within the documentation team.

New documentation presentation layer or user interface updates

The way online content looks or feels to users can change when the documentation tools change. For example, content tagging and/or formatting can be affected. You might need to review and update content accordingly. Updated tools can also make new formatting or presentation options, such as collapsible elements, available for a writer's consideration.

Errors or other clarification needs

Your primary engineering or product team, support engineers, another product team, or your documentation colleagues might point out errors or areas needing clarification in existing content. This can happen for a variety of reasons. You might discover simple typos or instances of information being lost in translation, so to speak, between engineering, product management, and docs when a feature was documented initially. In other situations, more information can surface about a feature as time passes. Limitations and dependencies that might not have been considered at development time can require documentation updates. It is also possible for a writer to re-open an investigation into an existing feature and discover gaps that need to be filled. You might, for example, discover that you need to discuss some of the feature's behavioral details that you did not initially deem necessary.

Other kinds of atrophy

It is beneficial to refresh content regularly, even when all the above reasons do not apply. Whenever you make updates for any of the other reasons mentioned here, treat that as an opportunity to look at the material as a whole and consider broader or more thorough updates. When existing content is carried over for many releases, topics can grow stale or brittle. Topics or manuals in which content has been mostly static for more than a few releases are likely due for maintenance consideration. When you can, check these topics for signs of documentation atrophy.

Symptoms of documentation atrophy can include the following.

- Topics that have grown too long and/or complicated with "patch" additions over several releases
- Wordiness or other style issues that make instructions or other information difficult to parse. This issue is worth considering especially when writing for an international audience.
- Excessive linking to other content, or, conversely, insufficient linking to related content.
- Heading structures that do not organize the content effectively.

When you revisit material that you haven't worked on for a while, new ideas and connections can occur to you. Your expertise can grow over time or use cases can change or merit reconsideration. When you look at material with a fresh eye you can often see its faults in a way that you couldn't when you wrote it up originally.

How to make updates

Assessing scope

When an update or maintenance need arises, it is a good idea to pause and reflect on the scope or impact of the change that you expect to make. The type of updates that you make to documentation can vary widely, from a simple change in the default value of some setting to a multi-topic set of additions that cover some significant new product feature. In between are more typical, and more problematic updates: changes that are a paragraph or two in length that deal with, for example, some previously undisclosed behavior or some enhancement to an existing product feature.

Handling updates with a moderate scope: to patch or not to patch?

Moderately sized updates can be problematic because their scale and scope are not always obvious. Let's consider an example.

A feature update to the user interface might add several configuration options previously available only as manual settings made in a configuration file system. Your existing content might include a table with names and descriptions for the manual configurations. How should you approach documenting the new user interface capabilities?

You might be tempted simply to patch such an update into the existing material, adding a sentence, screenshot, paragraph or a section, as the case may be, and then leave it at that. Frequently, such an approach is fine and valid. But just as frequently, it creates new problems for both writer and reader.

One reason is that scale dictates structure. That is, the structure that works for presenting a body of information with, for example, three main points might fall apart when the information is expanded to cover five points. Where you could easily discuss the three points in a single section, you might find that a single section is no longer sufficient for the expanded material. Perhaps you now need to rethink the structure and put each point in its own section.

Going back to our example, it might not be enough to keep the table with configuration setting names and descriptions and add a paragraph to mention that they are now available in the user interface. Consider the wider user experience implications of the feature update. The audience for this area of the product has likely evolved to include users who are not familiar with using configuration files. The process of making the configurations in the user interface is likely part of a new workflow within the product. Use cases and scenarios for this updated functionality should be considered. These impacts to the product, audience, and to user experience suggest that the topic needs to be reorganized and the content expanded.

Considering update impacts beyond your content: always a good idea

A second reason why updates that appear to be confined to one specific area of the documentation can cause problems is that they often also affect other parts of the documentation. Discerning such interdependencies can be difficult. For example, say you discover that a particular component in a networked system requires its own machine, where the previous recommendation was simply to colocate it with some other component. Your immediate solution might be to simply update an existing topic on setting up that component, in which you now state that the component needs to reside on its own machine.

But you must also consider what other material might need updating to incorporate this recommendation. Perhaps there are other topics that another writer handles which discuss how to build the entire system from the ground up. Or there's a manual on capacity planning, which discusses how to determine requirements for the entire system. Will you remember to tell the writers of those manuals about the need to put the component on a separate machine, so that the other content also gets updated? Unfortunately, if you're typical, there's a very good chance you won't even consider the possibility of changes outside your immediate scope, let alone take the steps to ensure that the necessary updates occur. So, don't be typical!

Sometimes a simple change in one place can have a cascading effect on multiple topics throughout a manual set. You must be aware of such possibilities. If you have been working in that area of the documentation for a while, you probably will be. But if you haven't been, it is useful to conduct audits of the documentation for each update you make, to ensure that your changes don't have impacts that you are not aware of. Even if you are very familiar with some subject and its documentation, you still must remember to look through the documentation closely to locate any corollary material that might need updating and then either make the changes yourself or inform other writers of the need for updates.

For example, a writer makes a change in a topic, in response to a product manager's request, to specify that a particular security setting is required, not optional. The writer is an expert on security issues, but knows little about the component or the content that covers it. The writer working on that component then looks at the change and knows immediately that there are nine other places in the content set that also describe the setting as optional, because the setting occurs in multiple procedures for deploying and configuring the component. So, it turns out that 10 changes were required, not one. Content reuse capabilities and structured authoring can mitigate some of this impact, but are no substitute for collective intelligence.

Regardless of the scope of the change to a feature, writers should always consider dependencies between the updated feature and other areas of the product. Other documentation content might be affected by even the smallest of changes, so it is advisable to consult with documentation colleagues working on related areas of the product. Notes, cautions, examples, and screenshots might need to be revised in topics that depend on the one you are updating. Links between different topics might also need attention. Read PRDs and ERDs (or other internal documentation) closely and talk to the product manager and developers to understand the full impact of any update.

Planning updates

As a rule of thumb, and all else being equal: update frequently. Make updating a major part of your process. Do not neglect the state of your existing material, even though you need to focus on new feature documentation at the same time.

Remember: the attention that you pay to updating existing content is what sets great documentation apart from the merely adequate.

Although frequent updates are important to facilitate the healthy evolution of documentation, you do need to consider certain factors when planning your updates.

Publishing tools

Your publishing tools can impose restrictions on your ability to update material. Perhaps your publishing process is burdensome, requiring transformation between the writing format and the publishing format or requiring close coordination among groups, such that you can only publish updates at the same time as new product releases.

Other types of publishing simplify and encourage the process of frequent updates. For example, wiki-based documentation can be updated instantly, allowing you to fix problems and respond to customer requests immediately, if need be.

Update types and timing

The timing of some updates is obvious. Documentation for a new or changed feature needs to appear in the version of the documentation that corresponds to the product version.

Updates stemming from customer feedback, missing content, or discovered errors should occur as soon as possible.

When style guidelines or product terminology change, writers often incorporate these revisions into other documentation work, making style or terminology changes in any topic that they update. Follow the recommendations of editors or managers for handling these kinds of updates.

Then there are categories of updates that are neither for new features nor for correcting significant content errors, such as those that clarify or expand on existing points. These can sometimes require significant time and planning; for example, if you decide to rearchitect a content set or split an existing manual into multiple documents.

Planning for major updates

Step back before diving in

If you need to make significant updates to content, such as a manual overhaul or other major reorganization, create and publish or share a documentation plan before starting on changes. Use the documentation plan to work out the bigger picture and clarify the goals that you have for the updates. It is often better to step back in this way before digging into the content. Significant maintenance updates can involve some tangles and you have to evaluate the degree to which you can risk leaving released content in an intermediate state, depending on how much other projects call you away from this work and on your publication process.

Another benefit to making a documentation plan for big updates is that you can break the project into discrete parts that do not compromise content stability as you complete each part.

Last, but not least, doc plans let you vet proposed updates with your scrum team and with documentation colleagues in advance. Socialize your plans and get input from product managers, engineers, and other colleagues if you can. They might be able to share insights, relay relevant user requests or feedback, or suggest solutions for particularly tricky content issues. They can also warn you of dependencies or other things that you should consider as part of the project.

In addition to making a doc plan, it might be possible to isolate a draft or "sandbox" version of the content in a restricted or unreleased documentation space. Making changes in this way frees you to experiment with organization and content without destabilizing the customer experience.

Syncing major updates with product release timing

Check with your managers and your team about timing larger updates to coincide with releases or other development milestones. Consider how a major content change will affect users and whether you can combine a major maintenance update with release-oriented work. It might be best to reserve significant updates for major software releases, rather than maintenance or patch releases.

Finding time for major updates

It can be challenging to find time for major maintenance updates while feature development and day-to-day maintenance tasks continue. Resist discouragement and look for opportunities wherever you can find them. Hack weeks, if your company holds them, can be an excellent time to hunker down and make innovative changes to existing content and to try new approaches to information design. Sign your project up for hack week; share your goals and results with the rest of the participating organization. Highlight the benefits you are delivering to internal and external customers by working on the project.

If hack weeks are not a possibility and you don't otherwise have a week or two to focus on a major overhaul, break a larger project into smaller parts. With your manager's approval, block off some time on your calendar to focus regularly on part of the project. Set expectations with colleagues about your availability or accessibility during this time. Of course, don't neglect important release work, customer interactions, or other needs that can't wait. In most cases, even the busiest writers can find an hour or two each week to devote to maintenance work without sacrificing other responsibilities. Chip away at the project as you are able. Recruit help if you need it. Favor stable and manageable iterations over an ambitious but unfeasible large single overhaul.

Conclusion

Content maintenance should be an important and frequent item on every writer's to-do list. It is an essential tool for building and sustaining customer trust. It is also a great way for writers to deepen their product knowledge and continually refine the informational and organizational machinery or architecture that underpins any content. In content maintenance, writers can put their investigative, disruptive, creative, and user-serving instincts to use, just as much as in new feature documentation.

Rewrite sentences, move or cut paragraphs, or reconsider whether a topic, chapter, or manual really works as-is. Stay on the lookout for brittleness, atrophy, or other dysfunction, and tinker boldly. Use what you know about your customers to focus on lean and relevant content. Embrace and initiate evolution to better serve users and keep your docs nimble.

10. Measuring Success

Everyone talks about metrics. We know they are important for building a business case for infrastructure improvements, demonstrating documentation team productivity, evaluating customer satisfaction, and more. There have been excellent articles and conference presentations about what to measure, and the value of doing it.

The metrics we hear most about in our profession are those that are reported by content management systems. Content management metrics certainly have value, especially for larger companies that have invested heavily in XML-based tool chains. They can provide information about return on technical investment, content reuse, and, to a certain degree, the amount of collaboration among writers.

But there are fundamental questions that every organization has to answer about whether to measure, what to measure, and how to do it. You have to start by understanding what measurement really means for a business, and then you have to decide what success looks like for your organization, and what criteria you care about.

Measurement

Too often, when we think about measurement, we think about precision. This habit of mind arises because we establish our thinking about measurement in terms of the physical world: from construction, cooking, or medicine. In those contexts, we measure precisely because there are physical consequences if we cut the board too short, add too much baking soda, or prescribe the wrong dosage.

Measurement in the less-tangible world of business is admirably clarified by Douglas Hubbard. His book *How to Measure Anything* argues eloquently that the purpose of measurement is to *reduce uncertainty so that you can make a decision based on the results.*[4] In other words: measurement is not about precise counting, and measurement has to support a business decision.

Reducing uncertainty is a liberating idea when you think about measurement. You can greatly reduce uncertainty about a question through estimation and small sample sizes. In most cases, doing the extra work required to reach a greater level of precision won't reduce uncertainty so much more that it is worth the effort. Don't make assumptions about the results, and don't overcomplicate the questions you're asking. Run small, simple experiments. Repeat them often. Refine your approach as you learn more from the measurements you take.

One example of this kind of simplicity is what Douglas Hubbard calls "The Rule of Five," which states that there is a 93.75% chance that the median of a population is between the smallest and largest values in any random sample of five from that population (Hubbard, 30). So, for example, if you want to determine how much time writers spend in meetings each week, you can just randomly sample five writers in your department. Take the highest and lowest responses you get: let's say five hours and 17 hours. The Rule of Five indicates that there is a 93.75% chance that the median number of hours the writers in your department spend in meetings is between five and 17 hours. Is this precise? Not at all. But it doesn't have to be in order to provide useful information. There are additional methods you can apply to reduce the uncertainty further, but think about how much you learned by making a quick survey of five people. You know that the median amount of time writers spend in meetings is probably between five and 17 hours a week. It's not as high as 25, it's not as low as two. If you are trying to implement changes to recover writing time, you can implement a new process and quickly survey five people again. If the range for the median moves down, you are

---

[4] *How to Measure Anything*, Douglas Hubbard, John Wiley and Sons, 2010, p. 6.

probably experiencing some success. You didn't have to survey the whole department, you didn't have to implement a time-tracking system, and you didn't have to worry about arriving at a "true number." You made a quick measurement, you ran a process experiment, you measured again, you evaluated your success, and you made adjustments. Measurement supports iteration.

If you are using estimation and small samples to reduce uncertainty, make sure you are applying these methods for a practical purpose. If you're not going to make a change based on the results, don't bother trying to measure it. Many organizations measure things because they can, without a plan to follow up with an action if the results go up or down. Your measurements should always support a business decision. First figure out what decisions you want to make, then decide which measurements can inform those decisions.

Measuring success

To measure success, you must decide what success means for your organization. There are many dimensions to the question, and no universal answer or set of answers. Think about what matters to your organization and what you want to optimize for. Content reuse? Quality? Customer satisfaction? Productivity? Efficiency? Innovation? Do you want to take a balanced scorecard approach, or are there one or two success criteria that are essential for your department?

You might have differing but complementary definitions of success within your department and in how you report to external constituents. Content reuse might be an important metric within your department because you are interested in resource allocation and consistency, while your upper management might be interested in content reuse in terms of localization savings and ROI on your content management system. Similarly, the productivity metrics that you track for performance management purposes might also be used by your business unit for resource planning.

The very idea of "success" is contextual. You must establish a clear definition of what constitutes success within your department and across your company. Then use measurement to reduce your uncertainty about those aspects of your success criteria that you will use to make informed decisions about what to change.

Mark Baker, author of *Every Page is Page One*, says that mean time to productivity is the only true measurement of whether documentation is successful or not.[5] That's another good example of something that would very hard to measure, even if you staged a formal user research program with customer site visits. But philosophically, he's right. The true purpose of your documentation is to educate your customer about how to use your products, either while they are learning about it or using it to do their tasks. The faster your documentation makes your customers productive, the more successful it is.

The classic metric for the success of technical documentation is support case deflection. It's an enticing metric because it promises to demonstrate monetary value for documentation. You know what the average cost of a support case is, so if you can figure out how many support cases the documentation deflects, you can make a reasonable estimate of how much company money the doc team is saving.

Unfortunately, support case deflection is a surprisingly difficult metric to capture, because it involves the measurement of an absence of action. Even the most sophisticated case studies of this metric acknowledge that at some point in your methodology, you just have to make a whopping assumption. As DB Kay & Associates concede in their white paper, "Close Enough: Simple Techniques for Estimating Call Deflection": "It's not possible to measure precisely, but executives want credible numbers anyhow."[6] The methodology they propose is to survey customers

---

[5] Mark Baker, personal communication, 2009.
[6] "Close Enough: Simple Techniques for Estimating Call Deflection", DB Kay & Associates,

directly and ask them whether their last interaction with the company web site was successful or resulted in them opening a support case. If the customer was successful and did not open a case, the survey would ask them to hypothesize whether they would have opened a case if they hadn't been successful. Surveys such as these provide some useful data. But it would be difficult to make an informed business decision based on anecdotal information with such a high degree of inference. Some companies try to reach a greater degree of certainty using click stream analysis. Here, too, inference plays an essential role:

> They do this by assigning a probability of success to different patterns of behavior. For example, a search with no results presented or clicked might have a zero probability of being successful, where a search with one or two clicks to results, followed by leaving the site, might be 75% likely successful (DB Kay & Associates, p. 7).

Clicking to results and then leaving the site without filing a case might represent a successful case deflection. It could also represent the customer giving up, asking a colleague for help, being interrupted to work on another task, or leaving the site to look for information on community forums. To account for those possibilities, the authors of the paper assign a 25% probability. Why 25%? They don't explain this detail of their methodology. They just make a whopping assumption. It does help reduce uncertainty, but it still produces pretty uncertain results.

Others have taken a more nuanced approach, and in the process can discover that their efforts to measure support case deflection were more valuable in answering a different question they hadn't thought to ask. See, for example, this excellent discussion from

---

http://www.dbkay.com/files/DBKay-SimpleTechniquesforEstimatingCallDeflection.pdf, p. 1.

Oracle in their white paper, "Measuring Search Success and
Understanding Its Relationship to Call Deflection":

> The customer support department of a large electronic design
> automation (EDA) software company wanted to track the
> relationship between caseload and support revenue. Before it
> turned on Web-based knowledge access, the slope of the
> caseload trend was a perfect match to the slope of the
> support revenue trend. For every new customer gained, the
> department's revenue and caseload went up at the same ratio.
> Once customers were granted access to Web-based
> knowledge, the slope of the caseload trend changed. Over a
> four-year period, the caseload went from around 6,000 cases
> per month to approximately 5,000. During this same period,
> revenue continued to grow. The slopes of the caseload and
> the revenue trends were no longer parallel because access to
> Web-based knowledge had caused them to diverge.
>
> Did call deflection occur in this case? Yes, it did. But it was
> nearly impossible to determine exactly how much had
> occurred. Over a four-year period, cases had decreased by
> 16.7 percent, so the deflection rate could be said to also be
> 16.7 percent. But that does not account for a simultaneous 40
> percent increase in support revenue. Projecting the caseload
> as if it were still tied to the revenue trend results in
> approximately 8,400 cases per month. Because the support
> department was registering only 5,000 cases, does this mean
> that calls were deflected at a rate of 40 percent? The 40
> percent number seems high, but the 16 percent number
> seems low. As you can see, determining the exact call
> deflection rate is difficult. Regardless of the exact call
> deflection percentage, the good news is that the department's
> workforce did not have to grow by 40 percent to cover the 40

percent increase in cases. The department deflected future spending, even if it did not reduce actual spending.[7]

Notice in this case that the authors don't reach a great degree of precision. They are using measurement properly and seem to settle on a case deflection somewhere between the boundaries of 16% and 40%. That's still a wide range, but they could apply some complementary measurements to narrow the range. What is genuinely interesting here is that they gained a significant insight that they appear to be deflecting future spending. This metric is something they could use to help them plan hiring and headcount allocation, even though it wasn't the result they expected to get from their measurement in the first place.

A different way to try to establish the financial value of your documentation is to ask your customers what they think it's worth. A group at Microsoft did this: they surveyed a significant number of Microsoft MVPs and asked them what they thought the value of the documentation was, as a percentage of the price of the software.[8] Entirely subjective, to be sure, but it provided some compelling information that enabled that documentation group to argue for a better percentage of the engineering budget to fund their content improvement efforts. If you have direct access to your customers, and you apply the Rule of Five, you can quickly gather some relevant business information, especially if you follow up by asking those customers to suggest what they think would make your documentation worth a higher percentage of the purchase

---

[7] "Measuring Search Success and Understanding Its Relationship to Call Deflection," Oracle white paper, November 2011, http://www.oracle.com/us/products/applications/measure-search-call-deflect-wp-1354584.pdf, pp. 4-5.

[8] Alan Theurer and Barbara McGuire, "Content and the Bottom Line: Defining the Business Value of Your Publications," Center for Information-Development Management Best Practices Conference, 2008.

price. Then do a similar quick study after you make some changes and your customers have had the time to absorb them.

At Splunk, we focus on customers first. We want to know if they think our topics are useful for them, which topics they read the most (and least), how long they spend on the pages, and how they navigate the site. Based on those customer analytics, we can make decisions about where to invest our time and resources. We gather this information through Google Analytics and the use of our own products, which enable us to index, search, and correlate a variety of disparate data from our web site, support portal, and internal systems. The combination of these two tools gives us insight into customer demographics, content usage, and customer satisfaction, as well as performance of our authoring platform, contributions to the documentation, and more.

Here, for example, is a Splunk report that shows the number of topics with the most "no" votes on our feedback form, correlated with the number of page views over a 12-month period:

uri_path	views	nos
/Documentation/MintAndroidSDK/latest/DevGuide/Requirementsandinstallation	13352	5
/Documentation/Splunk/latest/Data/Uploaddata	4613	4
/Documentation/SplunkLight/latest/GettingStarted/Aboutaddingdata	11688	4
/Documentation/WAS/2.0.1/User/WebSpherebasics	10215	4
/Documentation/Splunk/6.2.0/Security/SecureSplunkWebusingasignedcertificate	3445	3
/Documentation/Splunk/6.2.3/SearchTutorial/Aboutthesearchapp	9413	3
/Documentation/Splunk/latest/ReleaseNotes/MeetSplunk	70644	3
/Documentation/SplunkLight/latest/GettingStarted/StartSplunkLightandlogintoSplunkWeb	5452	3
/Documentation/SplunkLight/latest/Installation/InstallonLinux	8880	3
/Documentation/ActiveDirectory/1.2.2/DeployAD/EnableauditingandPowerShellondomaincontrollers	5409	2
/Documentation/AddOns/latest/CiscoASA/Description	11198	2
/Documentation/AddOns/latest/MSSQLServer/About	7217	2
/Documentation/AddOns/latest/MSSQLServer/Configuremodularinput	2319	2
/Documentation/AddOns/latest/Nessus/Description	7454	2
/Documentation/AddOns/latest/NetFlow/Overview	6207	2
/Documentation/AddOns/released/Overview/Singleserverinstall	5925	2
/Documentation/ES/latest/Install/Networkdashboard	581	2

See that second item: although the "Upload data" topic received four "no" votes over the past year, which is a high number, the page views are much lower than the release notes "Meet Splunk" topic, which received three "no" votes. Looking only at vote counts, or only page views, does not enable you to focus your remediation efforts properly. By correlating the two metrics, you can make an intelligent business decision that will improve valuable content for dissatisfied customers.

In this example, note the things discussed earlier:

- Although we are counting page views as well as "no" votes, we are not using those tallies to mean something on their own. *Counting is not measurement.*

- Although the numbers of "no" votes are small, we can still use them to gain insight we didn't have before about what the unvoiced opinions might look like. *Even small samples can reduce uncertainty.*

- Correlating these two tallies indicates where we can best apply efforts to improve content. *Measurement results in action.*

In an organization that focuses on customer success, we can use even rough measurements like these to guide our efforts.

So, as you respond to requests from upper management for more metrics, make sure you are measuring intelligently. Define what's important to your department and the company. Identify a set of business decisions you want to make. Figure out what you can measure to reduce the uncertainty involved in making those decisions. Run some small, easy experiments, and then adjust your measurements accordingly. Then report and take action. If you do this well, your department will be more successful and you might end up teaching upper management a thing or two about what it means to measure success and how to do it.

11. Research for Technical Writers

Telling me how my car works does not help me drive it. Tell me how to drive the car and why to drive it that way.

To write technical documentation that informs and explains, you need (1) some background about the technical field, (2) an approach to digging the salient facts out of the software and your sources, and (3) a way to express the meaning of those facts. This chapter proposes a journalistic approach to research that starts with this end in mind: documentation that provides fact and meaning in a way that is natural to the technical field.

The following problematic excerpt comes from an in-print user guide, with product references obscured to protect the vendor.

The FernBern Database is checked every two minutes for records that are added, edited, and deleted. If record updates are detected, the records are loaded (or reloaded) by the interface as appropriate. The two-minute update interval can be adjusted with the /updateinterval command-line parameter. The interface will only process 25 record updates at a time. If more than 25 records are added, edited, or deleted at one time, the interface will process the first 25 records, wait 30 seconds (or by the time specified by the /updateinterval parameter, whichever is lower), process the next 25 records, and so on.

Once all records have been processed, the interface will resume checking for updates every 2 minutes (or by the time specified by the /updateinterval parameter). All record edits are performed in the following way: old versions of edited records are deleted from the interface; new versions are added in. With some BerningMan Servers, this operation can require more time and more system resources. Therefore, it is more efficient to stop and restart the interface if a large number of records are edited.

It tells you how the software works, not how to solve your real-world problems. To reframe this information so that it addresses your concerns, you need to ask the right questions:

- What's the advantage? Why might I want to check for changes more frequently?
- What's the cost? If I check for changes more frequently, is performance of the interface affected? Is more memory or disk or CPU consumed? How much more? What's the effect on the performance of the target server if I increase the frequency?
- Security: Who can change the setting? Is some level of privilege required?
- Guidance: Exactly how many record changes make it efficient to bounce the interface?

What *are* the right questions? It depends on who your intended audience is. We're talking about performance and system resources here, so the reader is likely a system administrator, and you can assume they know something about tuning parameters. Equipped with the answers to these questions, you can tell them what to do and why to do it:

By default the interface checks for and processes record changes every two minutes. If your records change at a rapid rate (1000 changes or more per minute) and you require your BerningMan Server to remain as up to date as possible with changes to records, you can check more frequently by setting the updateinterval parameter to a lower value. To change the setting, you must be a FernBern interface administrator.

Be advised that more frequent checks increase the workload on the target BerningMan Server, because the interface sends updates more frequently. If you need to process more than

25,000 record changes an hour, you can increase the throughput of the interface by restarting it hourly.

Now you know how to keep your BerningMan Server current, and the price of doing so. How do we prepare to write this way?

First, do your background research

When embarking into a new technical field, take some time at the outset to scan the territory, get some context and learn the essentials. You don't need to become an expert, but you must come to the residents of the technical field: they will not come to you, and common sense alone will not save you. In addition to the technical side, research the business side: what's the business case for the project? Who is on it? What design documentation exists? How is the project being tracked online?

Here is one writer's anecdote about this:

As a programmer quite innocent of accounting principles, I was once confronted with a very unhappy customer, an enrolled agent using a module that I'd coded. He complained "This debit account: when I debit it, the total goes down." I said "OK. So what's the problem?" He repeated himself: "When I debit it, the total goes down." I said "Wait: when you debit a debit account, it's supposed to go up?" Exasperated, he said "Of course!"

Everyone knows that "debiting" means decreasing, right? Not necessarily true in accounting, it turns out: it depends on the type of account. Technical fields have their own language and usage, and to be accurate and understood, we must write for those experts in their language.

At that moment, of course, he lost any confidence he might have had in me and I realized that good faith and the ability to write code were not going to cut it: I needed to know accounting. I did take several accounting courses and read some books, not enough to become an expert but enough to provide a basis for the work I was hired to do.

Years later I worked at a large company that created interfaces to gather data from a wide variety of devices using all sorts of protocols, some decades old and specific to industries such as power generation or industrial device control. There is a world of industrial standards I'd never even heard of – OPC, S88, Modbus, and more. Assigned to rewrite some aging guides for these interfaces and chastened by my experience with debit accounts, I spent some quality time searching the Web and reading up on the standards before attempting to interview my sources. Said reading turned to be essential: the S88 standard, for example, describes a hierarchy that a computer-literate person might reasonably assume was a simple stack of parents and children, but it turns out to be deeply married to how manufacturing systems allocate equipment. This fact deeply informed all the conversations I subsequently had about how the corresponding interface composed an S88-compliant history of manufacturing runs.

Find out why your company is pursuing this project. What is the business case for it? If specifications, project web pages, and reputation slides exist, read them, and consider helping to write them: they are essential documents and your writing prowess can help ensure that they are clear and complete. If the project is tracked in an issue-tracking system like JIRA, monitor the project for changes and watch the issues. Know who is on the project team, and introduce yourself to the team.

Determine the truth

Write from primary sources. Determine what your reader needs to know and verify it yourself as much as possible. If you can't put your hands on it, cross-check it with multiple sources. Compose questions carefully and deliver them effectively.

Very embarrassing: ask a developer how a feature works, only to be asked in return "Did you try it?" You didn't. There is strong potential here for a loss of credibility with your sources: you risk looking lazy or, even worse, lacking in technical acumen, which is the coin of the realm.

Try it first. If this means digging for access to software, do so. The results can be interesting: in documenting the setup for one particular component, you might find three different user interfaces shipping simultaneously on three different platforms, because three different developers in three different groups solved the same problem in slightly different ways.

When writing procedures, perform a step and then write it immediately. Report it as it happens. There is a testing aspect to this, too: try making likely mistakes and seeing what happens. If the software does not handle errors gracefully, file defects.

As a reporter, you need to be an adept interviewer. Ask the right people the right questions the right way.

Who are the right people? Talk to the developer who is responsible for a feature, but also the product manager. Ask your PM about the user goals that the software is intended to address. Consider pulling in a Support person and QA engineer. If they disagree, get them in the same room and broker a conversation. Don't cast your net too wide or you'll never finish writing, but do go beyond the originating developer. Developers tend to talk about how a feature is implemented (how the car works), so ask them about the implications of the implementation. Talk to customers if you have access to them. Nothing builds understanding and empathy more than direct conversation with the people who use your products every day.

What are the right questions? Ask the questions that answer what your readers need to know. Your standard questions will depend on your technical field and there will always be situation-specific questions, but here are some essential questions for software products:

- Settings: What's the default? Minimum? Maximum? Are there magic numbers? What does 0 (zero) do? What about -1? Zero is a magic number in software. It might stand for a default value, for example, when it would be better to make that default visible. It also sometimes means zero, in fact, in a situation where specifying zero for a setting made no sense and was even problematic. There is virtue in a UI that hides magic numbers from users: it's fine to store 0 or -1 for a setting in a configuration file, but the user interface can provide a check box or radio button labeled with a precise meaning, eliminating the need to document a magic number.

- Is security a consideration? Is a particular level of privilege required to perform a task or access a feature?

- Is performance affected by an option or setting? What about resource consumption?

- Can data integrity be jeopardized or can the user somehow endanger the integrity of their installation in the execution of a task?

What's the right way to ask a question? There are two aspects to this: the mode of delivery and the framing of the question itself.

- **Choosing a delivery mode**: Ask your sources "What's the best way for me to work with you? Email? Chat? Face to face? Phone?" Respect their preference as long as it works. However, if they say "Email, please" and then don't respond to email, find a mode to which they do respond. There is an advantage to getting answers in fixed form (email or chat), because you have the history of the conversation. Chat is great for quick answers, less so for long, detailed exchanges.

Consider using your issue tracking system to conduct the conversation—it's a very collaborative mode and all interested watchers are likely to see your question. If you interview in person or on the phone, be sure to take notes, write them up, and send them to the source to confirm that you heard them correctly.

- **Framing the question**: What kind of answer do you need? To get an unambiguous answer, ask a simple question, the simpler the better. Can it be a yes or no question? To get a discursive answer, do the opposite: ask an open-ended question. For quick response, ask one question at a time, as opposed to batching them, unless your source prefers you to do so.

- **Who wants to know?** If your source doesn't know who you are, tell them. If you work in different locations, it's probably worth telling them where you're located, too. Consider telling them why you're asking the question, if you think it will help your source frame an appropriate answer: "We're planning to adapt the enterprise user documentation for cloud customers, so I'd like to know...."

When asking questions, set a collaborative tone. Questions in email and chat can come across as confrontational, even when you don't intend them to be. Prefer "we" to "you," which can come across a bit accusatory: "When we say..., do we mean...?" Send the message that the whole team has a stake in the documentation.

Even when a question is well-framed and properly delivered, it can be hard to get a timely answer. Sources are busy, and your questions are probably not their priority. After a decent interval, ask again. Be as cheerfully persistent as a golden retriever. Give them a deadline. When the direct approach does not work, you can sometimes provoke a response by writing something that is so wrong that a reviewer will be compelled to respond. When reviewers see something in fixed form, they tend to react as if it were already set in stone. Fine, as long as they respond with the correct information!

Convey the meaning of it all

Address the concerns of the technical field, use the language of the reader, and watch for hidden meaning.

In any technical field, there will be a set of first principles that are dear to the denizens of the technical field. Address those concerns. For example, QA engineers writing unit tests want those tests to be:

- Fast
- Independent
- Repeatable
- Self-checking
- Timely

So, if you're documenting a tool for unit test developers, tell them how to use your product features for maximizing speed, insulating tests from each other, and so on. Note side effects: feature x increases speed but decreases accuracy.

In writing about a technical field that is new to you, pay close attention to terminology:

- Watch out for jargon. The way people talk is not necessarily the way we want to write. Ask whether a term is standard for the industry, and omit jargon from your writing.

- Use terminology accurately. Assigned to document a COM API, a writer interviewed the developer, who kept talking about the methods "exposed" by the API. It sounded odd to an untrained ear, but turned out to indeed be the correct term. Knowledgeable readers would have been puzzled if the writer had contrived some other term based on inexperience.

- Watch for specialized meanings or nuances in the use of common words (like "debit," for example).

Beware the subjunctive, mainly "should"—it's a red flag for hidden meaning, expressing either a recommendation or a requirement. Are you making a recommendation? "You <u>should</u> set the maxreads parameter as close to 1000 as possible." Tell your reader why they want to do this and what they risk by doing or not doing it: "For highest accuracy, set maxreads as close to 1000 as possible. Be advised that increasing the maxreads setting by 100 increases the amount of disk I/O by 10%, which affects performance." To convey a requirement, use "must," and explain why.

What if they *do* need to know how it works?

Tell them, of course, and tell them why they need to know.

In any technical domain, there are a core set of concerns, so be sure to lead with them. If someone needs to know how a feature works in order to tune its performance, explain it in those terms, so they can configure it successfully. If someone needs to understand how a statistical algorithm is implemented before you can trust its output, you must explain it to them! The question to ask when deciding whether to explain implementation is "Why do they need to know?"

Consider doing nothing

Omit implementation details unless there are user-facing consequences. When confronted with oddities, see if the product can address them. Be honest, but be discreet.

Implementation can change, and, again, describing the engine doesn't help the driver. If, as a result of the implementation, there's an actionable consequence or meaningful restriction, include it and explain it: "The configuration is stored in a proprietary non-relational database format, which means you cannot use SQL queries to read or modify it."

Your research might turn up some oddities in the software. Before you blithely ensconce them in user documentation, ask a few questions:

- **Why is this thing odd?** Maybe there's a historical reason or a technical constraint that prevents a feature from being implemented in a more sensible way. It might not be wise to document the reason. Describe the essentials accurately and move on.
- **Can it go in the user interface?** Gracefully? Users prefer using the product, and recourse to the documentation is a distant second choice for them. If you find yourself documenting an elaborate manual process, ask whether it can be automated on behalf of the user.
- **Can the software know it?** If you're telling the user to enter information about the computer that they are using, for example, much of that information is probably readily available to the software. If you're warning the user about possible errors, can the software detect those errors and either prevent them or provide error messages? If so, there's no need to document them.

How forthcoming should you be? You need to balance the need of your readers for accurate essentials with their perception of your product—you certainly don't want to reduce their trust. You also need to assume that your competitors are reading your documentation. It can be useful to couch sensitive information in very bland wording: "To maximize performance..." or "To ensure optimal security...." Boring? Yes! But words like "performance" and "security" attract the attention of the skimming reader, and all our readers skim. And by no means do you want to expose a security risk in your product.

Say thank you!

Always and sincerely thank the people who help you, every time.

12. Scenario-driven Information Development

It is essential to document your product based on its concepts, features, and the procedures the users must follow in order to be successful. You might also have written an introductory tutorial to teach new users the basics of your product. To engage your users even more, consider enhancing your existing reference docs, conceptual explanations, procedural instructions, and tutorials with scenario-based documentation that addresses the problems and goals that brought them to your product in the first place.

Why use scenarios?
Scenarios provide customers with concrete examples of how they might use your product to solve problems they have in the real world.

- Users are not motivated to read about your product's features, only about how they can solve their problems. A well-written scenario keeps this motivation in mind and identifies product features only in the context of how they solve the problem posed in the scenario.
- Scenarios help bridge gaps in skill levels, from beginner to intermediate and intermediate to advanced. Conceptual overviews can be too broad, while procedures can be too detailed or specific.
- Scenarios can bring concepts and procedures to life by applying them to a real-world example that the user can relate to.

What is a scenario?
A scenario is an end-to-end walkthrough of a real-world example, using the product to solve a problem or achieve a goal that your audience cares about. For example:
- Monitor privileged user behavior by creating a dashboard
- Report on failed logins

- Track the bounce rate by product
- Integrate an information stream using the SDK

The goal is to help the user complete a complex task in a way that will solve a problem and help them tackle similar tasks in the future.

What isn't a scenario?

A scenario is not a tutorial, which walks the user through a rudimentary example to instruct them in basic concepts, tasks, and features of the product. A tutorial is the "hello world" of learning to code. A scenario explains how to solve a problem based on a real use case. It does not introduce a set of product features with a goal to instruct the user about them. Like a tutorial, a scenario can also be interactive so that users can follow along inside the product.

A scenario is also not a marketing case study, which can over-promise feature capabilities and offer elevated jargon around actual product functionality. While it can be closely aligned with marketing content, a scenario walks the user through a specific process while recognizing the limitations of the product. A scenario shouldn't explain how to do something with the product if the product isn't well-suited or designed to perform that task.

Finally, a scenario is not comprehensive product documentation. Because you are focusing on a single problem and walking through one end-to-end solution, it would be inappropriate to cover multiple paths through the product, or other adjacent items in the product that are not immediately relevant to the scenario. Give your customers a seamless path to the solution and leave variations, options, and all additional functionality out of the scenario. Your regular documentation will cover that material.

How to design a scenario

Step 1: Define your audiences

A successful scenario is pitched to a very specific persona. You want to be able to make it clear at the beginning of the scenario or use case which audience you've written it for, so each reader can quickly identify if this scenario fits his or her needs. With a well-defined audience for each scenario, you can make sure that all the procedures align to that specific persona. It's okay to link to more detailed tasks along the way, but the audience definition should determine the scope and level of detail of the scenario content. If you are not sure how to define your audience, write learning objectives for the scenario to help you sort out the audience you have in mind.

Defining your audience first will also help you plan for how many scenarios you need. If you have several distinct audiences that you want to serve, you might need to prioritize which audiences will benefit most from one or more scenarios.

As you consider your audiences, plan for the tone and style of your scenario documentation. Should the writing style be different, perhaps more personal or more casual and blog-like, than a typical documentation topic? Will your scenario be delivered with your other documentation offerings, or will it work better in a different delivery mechanism? Will your scenario include any unusual content that might introduce a different maintenance burden, such as a large number of screenshots, or sample files, or other media that need to be updated each time the product changes?

Step 2: Gather scenarios

Work with product managers, designers, and engineers to find out what kinds of scenarios and workflows are being built into the product (if any). Ask the team what use cases they are building certain features to support. As you gather this information, keep an eye out for scenarios or workflows that describe how a user is going to use your products. Rephrase any feature-driven workflows into a use case that describes the problem the customer wants to solve or the business need they are trying to fulfill.

The customer-facing teams in your organization are another excellent source for scenarios. Canvass all your customer feedback channels to determine what problems your customers are trying to solve, what common questions they have, and what they identify as their main pain points. Talk to sales, support, customer education, and professional services (on-site consulting) teams to learn more about what customers want to do with your product. Keep in mind that you might want to write multiple scenarios targeted at different audiences. Some might be based on a low-level use case focused on a single task, while others might present a high-level use case that touches many different aspects of the product.

You can also talk to product management and read their user stories if you're developing a scenario based on a bleeding-edge feature. Why was the feature developed? Use those stories to build your documentation around solving a real customer problem, demonstrating how using the feature is relevant to that solution.

Compile a list, then assess the target audience for each scenario to ensure your proposed scenarios correspond to the audiences that your product serves. Also consider the difficulty of documenting each scenario. How much information currently exists to support the scenario context? How much independent research would you need to flesh out the scenario? If you'll be taking screenshots, do you have available systems and sample data to populate the product in a realistic way? Eliminate any scenarios that do not fit your audience goals or that fall outside the parameters of what you can support.

Validate your refined list with product management, marketing, and customer-facing teams. If possible, validate the proposed scenarios directly with customers.

Step 3: Write the scenario

Start by articulating the work you have done already: define the audience and define the goal of the scenario. You might also need to set additional context or prerequisites to ensure that the user can follow along successfully with the end-to-end walkthrough. After you've defined the goal and stated any prerequisites, provide users with a specific starting point in the product. As you walk through the steps, continue to address your audience's goals in a way that leads with the goal and follows with the product, never the other way around.

Scenarios can include several tasks and procedures combined to support the scenario's stated goal. In the context of the scenario's narrative, you might ignore or highlight some optional tasks, depending on the learning objectives. Think of it as "practical railroading"—you are using a specific narrative context to guide the user to a particular understanding of and knowledge about the product in a way that the scenario illustrates and makes valuable to them.

Step 4: After you write the scenario

Validate the written scenario with QA to make sure that the documented workflow is well-supported and not error-prone. Your goal is a seamless experience, so if the scenario is causing the reader to stumble across bugs or difficulties, start a discussion with QA and product management about whether the product or the scenario need to be adjusted. You can also work with UX to determine if workflows can be built directly into the design of the product to improve the ease of performing the scenario.

Consider connecting your scenarios to marketing and education deliverables as an element of an integrated content experience. You can work with these teams to produce a more conceptual version to be used in marketing materials and a more hands-on version to be used in training classes. If marketing, education, and documentation all produce content around the same scenarios, the user receives clear and consistent information when they evaluate the product, ramp up with initial training, and continue to use it over time.

Solicit feedback from your readers. Track which scenarios are working well for users and which are less useful to them so that you can tailor them better.

For an entertaining and insightful discussion of writing engaging scenario-based docs for a highly technical product, see the video of Matt Ness's 2015 Write the Docs conference presentation, "Let's Tell a Story," available at:

https://www.youtube.com/watch?v=3hneCmLYWjc&feature=youtu.be

13. Technical Editing

Technical editing helps technical writers do their best writing. Technical editing instills consistency throughout a body of documentation, improves the overall quality of the docs, makes your content more accessible, ensures that content follows good information design principles, and trains writers to write well.

Having someone edit your writing makes it better. Here's the thing about bad technical writing: no one reads it. If a user lands on a topic in your documentation that is badly written, and it doesn't help them learn something or solve their problem, they will move on.

What is technical editing?

When you think about editing, you might think of your 10th grade English teacher and a very red pen. In the world of technical documentation, editors are content advisors. A writer should be able to go to their editor with a question they have about their writing (a question that the style guide doesn't cover), a grammar question, a product name question, to get feedback on a major reorg they are planning for legacy content, and so on. Technical editing covers a wide spectrum of writerly things that stretch far beyond catching typos, including: technical accuracy, grammar, style, punctuation, code review, usability, audience definition, and minimalism. Technical editing is all about supporting the writer as they develop content that is going to help the customer be successful.

Consistent style

Writing is hard. Writing well is even harder. Writing well consistently is even harder than that. Having multiple writers writing well consistently with consistency of style is the hardest of all. Technical editing is the keystone to achieving consistency of style throughout a body of documentation, especially when multiple writers contribute to that body of documentation. There's so much that can be said about style, and yet it's elusive. Writing is hard enough. Writing about writing? Forget it. How can a doc team achieve the same style across multiple content sets for different audiences written by many writers published through different delivery systems? How can a lone technical writer achieve consistent style from what they wrote in the morning to what they wrote after lunch? Technical editing can go a long way in helping individual writers and groups of writers write with consistent style in their documentation.

Editors are in a unique position to have an overall view of the content. Many doc teams are structured to align with the product development organization, which can lead to siloed content. Writers often work alone to produce the documentation for their own product area. Without a shared foundation of style rules, writers will produce documentation with varying styles. Technical editors can help reduce the variation in writing styles by creating a style guide for the documentation team, editing for style when writers submit their content for editing, and encouraging writers to adapt their writing to the style that is best suited to their audience.

The style guide

A lot of writers credit themselves with the ability to "write with house style" or to "write according to a style guide." So why do we need style guides, and why do writers need to have the ability to write according to them?

Style guides are another channel (besides editors) that can help establish consistency throughout a doc set. Writers can refer to the style guide when they have a question about their writing.

If your doc team has an editor or editors, it's likely that a big portion of their contribution will be creating a style guide. If your doc team doesn't have an editor or editors, it's likely that the early-hire writers and managers will create a style guide.

Style guides offer another huge advantage: they save time. On a well-functioning doc team, writers spend their time writing or increasing their knowledge of the product—not debating whether a file name should be in formatted in monospace font, or if you allow contractions in your docs. A style guide has answers to common content questions at the ready so that writers keep writing, instead of getting stuck on a style question or starting a controversial water cooler conversation about what capitalization scheme to use for headings.

Editing for style

Editing, especially editing for style, should not be too restrictive. Style isn't really something that you can establish rules for. In fact, style often comes from *breaking* rules. While it's great to have a style guide to cover issues that come up again and again, allowing some flexibility for style often lets you speak to your audience and let them know that robots aren't writing the docs, but real people who want to help them achieve success.

Editing for style is a fine line. You might be inclined to suggest a change just because you don't like the style with which another writer wrote a topic you're editing for them. Ask yourself if the style matches what your doc team is going for in their voice and tone. Ask yourself if the information is clear and accurate. It's easy to fall into the trap of rewriting someone else's content when you're editing for them.

Finally, it doesn't have to be perfect. Striving for perfection is admirable—and some people might argue that perfection is part of what editing is all about—but there is such a thing as over-editing. If you reorganize, rewrite, and comment on most of the content you were asked to look at, what's left? When you're editing, think about whether the content will be clear and helpful to the user. Be selective with your comments and focus on the items that really affect the goals of the content. Release cycles are getting faster and faster, and doc content doesn't have as long of a shelf-life as it used to. If the content gets the point across to the user, obsessing over an edit can delay content delivery, detract from the style of the doc, and ultimately do more harm than good.

You too can write with style

How can you learn to write with style? Reverse engineer good documentation. Find your favorite documentation and let it inspire you. Do you have opinions or strong feelings about the collective voice and tone of the docs your team produces? Get involved with the creation and maintenance of your doc team's style guide. Don't have time to develop your own style guide? Read style guides from doc teams at other companies. Many companies publish their style guides. Start with existing style guides such as the *Google Developer Documentation Style Guide,* the *Microsoft Writing Style Guide, The Chicago Manual of Style,* or the US Federal Government's *18F Content Guide.* Have a chat with your editor. Stay current with information development trends; attend meet-ups, read papers, read books about technical writing, attend conferences, etc. Finally, experiment! Write daringly and see what your editor has to say about it.

Quality assurance in content development

Technical editing helps to ensure linguistic and design quality in software documentation.

Writing with clarity, and without ambiguity, is one of the top ways to assure quality in your documentation. If your documentation is clear, your users will find the information they need to succeed in their tasks and solve their problems with your products. Technical editing ensures clarity in the documentation. Even if your doc team doesn't have editors, a peer edit or having someone else read your docs can help you determine if your content isn't clear.

Ensuring docs have good information design

Technical editors, like technical writers and doc managers, often find themselves in the role of information architect or content strategist. They can help a team develop information models or help a writer organize their documentation for usability.

It might sound simple, but often documentation needs editing in order to conform to the intended purpose of the topic.

Technical editors might help doc team members with such questions as:

- Who is the intended audience for this content?
- Does this information path lead the user through the content efficiently?
- Does this topic adhere to a topic type in our information model?
- Do we need a new topic pattern?
- How do you handle optional steps in a task?
- How do you organize conditional information?
- Is this topic too long?
- Should we delete this topic altogether?

Practical editing

Editing reassures some people and terrifies others. If your documentation team has editors or is considering bringing editors on board or even instituting peer editing, here is some practical advice about technical editing.

For editors

If you are editing content for someone, be objective and don't judge. Your job is to edit for clarity and style, not to rewrite or unilaterally reorganize a writer's content. Evaluate it for organization, usability, discoverability, relevance, and minimalism. Edit for clarity and style. Just because you wouldn't have written it the way they did doesn't mean it's not good writing.

Try to give the writers a solid foundation for working with editors. Support them by producing a style guide that they can trust and refer to with confidence while they are writing.

If you do create or maintain a style guide for your doc team, be prepared for requests to add things to it. Your team will rely on you to do the research and lead the effort on the decision around new guidelines. Also, be prepared for objections to style rules you establish. Issues such as whether to use the serial comma can cause major controversy on a documentation team. Make a decision, document it, and move on.

Writers often want to defend their writing and object to editorial suggestions you make about changing their content. Listening to a writer defend the choices they made while developing content is a great way to have a conversation about style and good writing practices. Explaining your edits is a good way to share your knowledge about industry standards or why certain style guidelines suit your company and audience. Have before-and-after meetings when you are working with a writer. Before the edit, have them explain to you what their goals were in writing the topic, what information they had to work with, and any legacy content issues they struggled with. After the edit, meet again to review your questions and highlight any recurring habits or issues you think the writer should attend to. And don't be offended if a writer chooses not to implement a change you suggest.

Sometimes people you work with will think you "just copyedit" or "just proofread" docs that other people write. If you run into someone who thinks this way, use the encounter as an opportunity to educate that person on what technical editors do and the value you bring to the company.

For edit-ees

When you receive edits on your content, don't take it personally. For substantive edits, try to keep an open mind about comments from your editor. It's highly likely that there is a reason they made the comment that they did. For non-substantive edits, don't rely on your editor to catch every error in your content. Try

123

not to judge them when they fail to catch a simple typo in your content. You can fix that yourself. Keep in mind that editors make mistakes too.

When you're writing, don't make up styles. Even if you work on a small team of writers, variations in style can proliferate quickly and ultimately make more work for your team to undo further down the road. If you find yourself unsure of how to write something, consult the style guide, talk to your editor, or if you work in a smaller department, discuss it with a peer writer.

For everybody

In the software industry, product releases are happening with ever-increasing frequency. Who has time for editing? Is editing a blocker for doc delivery in an Agile environment? What if you are working in a cloud services environment with continuous integration and continuous delivery? You might say, "My scrum team works in two-week sprints. Definition of done includes docs. How am I supposed to get my docs through not only tech review but also an edit within two weeks?"

Where does technical editing fit into the writing process in a fast-paced product development environment with frequent product releases? You might ask yourself, who has time to edit? Do I have to do it?

Editing is an *opportunity*. Of course you don't have to do it. Editing affords you an opportunity to deliver the best possible content that you can. When an editor edits technical content for a writer, they have the opportunity to support that writer in delivering high-quality content.

If your documentation team follows the practice of topic-based writing, encourage writers to request their edits for one or a few topics at a time. Processing content in smaller units means faster cycle time and will help your team keep up with the pace of software development.

One of the best things a writer or a doc team can do for their audience is deliver content that has been technically reviewed and edited. Would you publish a book you wrote without having it edited? Delivering doc that hasn't been edited is like giving a keynote speech at a big conference without testing the sound and presentation equipment. No one's writing is perfect. Are you sure that you've written technically accurate content for the correct audience with minimalism and a global readership in mind? Asked differently, why would you ever deliver documentation that *hasn't* been edited?

You wouldn't. You shouldn't. So don't. Get a second pair of eyes on everything you write.

14. Technical Verification

Among the key attributes of good documentation are accuracy and relevance. To ensure that your documentation is accurate, covers the important use cases, and provides sufficient detail so that the reader can accomplish all necessary tasks, the technical review phase is critical.

In particular, it is vital that your procedures undergo technical review and, in many cases, formal testing. Inaccurate or incomplete procedures waste the time of your users and have the potential to degrade their environments.

The technical verification process involves reviews of the documentation by subject matter experts (SMEs) and others. Where appropriate, it also includes formal testing of procedures by members of your quality assurance (QA) team.

A few guiding principles

This chapter discusses these key points:

- Technical reviews are vital to the accuracy of the documentation and, therefore, to the usability of the product.
- Reviews are non-negotiable. Reviewers must review, whether or not they have the time or inclination. Great documentation requires the participation of the entire product team, not just the writer.
- Reviewers have very little time to spend on your review, so the better you prepare your material for review, the better the results.
- You cannot accept poor or incomplete reviews.
- Formal testing of procedures is critical.
- The integrity of the review process is ultimately your responsibility.

Why is technical verification always necessary?

Adopt the premise that technical verification by someone other than you, the writer, is always necessary. You can carve out exceptions as needed, but start from the point of view that all your material requires verification. Your readers deserve it.

Technical verification is necessary for a number of reasons. We all have blind spots. It is difficult to review one's own documentation with complete care and thoroughness, even if, or rather, especially if, it is information that you are familiar with. Just as occasional typos slip through our writing, no matter how carefully we review it, so do the technical equivalent of typos. You might forget to include some prerequisite information. Or you elide a few steps in a procedure. Or you make unwarranted assumptions about your audience. The review provides the opportunity to uncover those blind spots by ensuring that additional eyes have a look at the material.

The SMEs that you rely on for information have blind spots too. They might neglect to mention certain aspects of the feature when you interview them. Or some of the information that they provided to you changes without notice. Or they might forget to update the engineering design documents that you rely on.

The technical review is particularly important when documenting non-GUI features, such as command line interfaces, APIs, and so on. GUIs serve to guide the user, often limiting the need for detailed instructions. They also serve to constrain the user, by restricting values or by performing validation checking, making it less likely that the user can go seriously astray. But when you document features that lack such interactive checks and a conscious visual design, inaccuracy or incompleteness in the documentation can lead to significant wasted time on the user's part. In addition, it is more difficult for you to verify your procedures when you do not have a GUI to work with. The importance of thorough technical review by third parties thus becomes that much greater.

Most importantly, procedures of a certain complexity or criticality should undergo formal QA testing. Good candidates for QA testing include procedures that involve distributed environments, where you have multiple pieces of software talking to each other. QA is already testing the software, and they can test the related documentation using their existing test beds. They are attuned to matters such as edge cases that you might not think to test for. Other procedures that warrant formal QA include any that take significant time to accomplish or that can potentially result in negative consequences, such as loss of data, if they are incorrect.

Who performs technical reviews?

When choosing your technical reviewers, be sure to account for all areas of your documentation that require verification. In addition to verifying the overall technical accuracy of the material, this is the time to confirm the validity of any use cases and to test the correctness of any procedures.

These are the main groups to consider as technical reviewers:

- SMEs. This group includes, first and foremost, the developers who worked on the feature and that you talked to during your research. It might also include other developers or other writers with overall expertise in the area that your feature addresses. The SMEs can assess the accuracy and completeness of your material.

- Product managers. The product managers drive feature development from the customer standpoint. In the absence of your own direct customer contact, they are often your most important link to the customer and are deeply knowledgeable about customer needs and issues. Product managers can provide valuable feedback on a number of issues, including your use cases and scenarios.

- Customer-facing personnel. Customer support, sales engineers, customer education, and professional services engineers have a great deal of insight into customer needs and, especially, customer pain points.

- The QA team. The people testing the feature code are among your best information sources. They are trained to approach their testing methodically and objectively. As such, they often discover issues, errors, and holes in the documentation that the SMEs overlook. In addition, testers are vital for one specific type of review: they are the only ones that can properly validate your procedures. QA testing of procedures is so important to the usability of your documentation that this chapter discusses it in great detail in a later section.

At times, it makes sense to include in your review additional, non-SME, developers, along with engineering managers, writers, and so on. Include anyone who might have unique insights to offer based on their areas of expertise.

For each review, distinguish clearly between those reviewers who are essential and those who are optional.

Types of reviews

Reviews can take many forms. These are some of the main types:

- Spot reviews
- Draft reviews
- QA reviews
- Review meetings

A spot review is generally a direct exchange with an SME to confirm your understanding of some feature or issue. Spot reviews are particularly effective when you are in the midst of writing about some feature, to ensure that your basic assumptions are correct. Spot reviews can occur through email exchanges, short meetings, online chats, and so on.

Draft reviews, along with QA reviews, are the most important type of review, and the type that this chapter addresses at length. A draft review is, as its name implies, a review of a draft of your document. These are written reviews—you send out a written draft or pull request, and your reviewers respond with written comments.

QA reviews are reviews of procedures by members of the QA organization. These reviews are can be critical to ensuring the usability and validity of your procedures.

Review meetings can be valuable, particularly if the results of your draft review are disappointing. They are also a great way to address discrepancies between reviews. They are, however, laborious. Furthermore, it can be difficult to keep the meeting focused on the documentation and to complete the review within the allotted time. For these reasons, it is often best to reserve review meetings for situations where the draft review produced poor results.

The next section of this chapter focuses on draft reviews, followed by a concluding section that covers QA reviews in depth.

When to do a technical review

Technical review is not a one-time event. Rather, verification of the validity of your documentation must be an ongoing and, in fact, a never-ending process. It begins when you start investigating a feature, and it continues to the point when the feature, and its documentation, are released to customers. But even then, you must continue to validate your material as you receive new information, customer and internal feedback, logged bugs, and so on. Both the product and its documentation live for a long time in the sustaining phase of their life cycle.

For now, we'll focus on the technical review process that precedes the release of a feature. These are the main times when content verification takes place:

• During the document development process. After you have conducted your preliminary research on a feature and have begun to write, you must continue to talk to the SMEs to ensure that you thoroughly understand what you are writing about. Do not wait until the review phase to get verification on difficult or unclear concepts, for example. If you wait too long, you are opening yourself up to the possible need for massive rewrites due to compounding errors and misunderstandings.

- After a draft is complete. At this point, submit the material for formal review by SMEs and other stakeholders, such as developers, product managers, technical support, and other writers.

- As a final step, submit your procedures for testing by the QA team to ensure that any complex or critical procedures are correct. We will discuss this important review element in detail later.

How to get a (good) review

The success of the review process sometimes seems sadly dependent on the whims and personalities of particular reviewers. Some SMEs are great reviewers, noticing all manner of detail and missing information. With others, their eyes glaze over as soon as they open your document on their screen. And many, if not most, reviewers are excellent at procrastination. So, one might ask, how to get a great review despite the best, or possibly the worst, intentions of your reviewers?

One factor that matters a lot, and is probably largely beyond your ability to affect, short of moving to a new company, is the established relationship between the doc team and the engineering team. Do the engineers view the writers as part of their team? Do they understand the importance of good documentation to product usability and customer satisfaction? Do engineers understand their responsibility for ensuring the quality of the documentation?

Another bedrock factor, which you *do* have a great deal of control over, is your own relationship to the engineering team. Do they see you as part of their team? Do they experience your contributions in a positive light? And, frankly, do they view you as smart or stupid? You can help your standing on a team considerably by showing that you're prepared and up-to-date on the feature work, by such actions as participating in the development meetings and reading and absorbing all relevant engineering documents before sitting down with the developer to discuss a product feature. Also, ask intelligent questions, make intelligent suggestions, and so forth. And, whatever you do, don't allow yourself to feel intimidated—or, if you do feel intimidated, don't allow it to show. See Chapter 17, "Working with Engineers," for more.

Whatever the state of these underlying factors, there is still plenty that you can do to improve the review process. Remember that the reviewers are generally going to spend as little time as possible on the review, and therefore, you want to make sure that they use that time well.

The following suggestions, listed by review phase, should help improve your review process.

Prepare the review

- Complete your own review first. Clean copy means no distractions. You don't want the reviewers to focus on your typos, which they will if there are any, instead of spending the time to do a content review. Review your writing and make it as clean and as clear as possible before you send material out for review.

- Communicate your review priorities. If you want the reviewers to focus on only a single section of a topic, let them know.

- Do not overwhelm reviewers with endless suggestions about how to do their reviews. Understand that they are going to spend as little time as possible on the review. Therefore, you need them to focus on the documentation and nothing but the documentation. If there's something in the documentation that requires further explanation, add a note to the reviewers in the copy itself. Don't distract your reviewers by asking them to absorb a lot of extraneous information about what constitutes a good review. They won't read it, anyway, so it's a waste of your time.

- Target your reviewers. Specify each person individually, and do not ask someone to review something if another reviewer is covering the same ground. For example, if there's one key engineer for a feature, that's the engineer who should review your material. Don't ask all the engineers or the engineering managers to review it as well. It's a great idea to provide courtesy notice to other interested parties, and common etiquette suggests that you do so in any case, but do your best to limit your list of required reviewers to the essential few. Nobody wants to feel that their time is not being respected. Furthermore, if you ask two engineers to review the same material, they will invariably each assume that the other is handling the review, and you will wind up with no review at all. Occasionally, you might need multiple engineers to look at the same material, particularly if neither is a very good reviewer, but, for maximum likelihood of success, schedule them sequentially rather than simultaneously.

• Make sure that each reviewer understands his or her role. If you need the product manager to review the use cases, for example, make that clear. It's great if they review the rest of the material as well, but tell them what you need them to focus on. Again, remember that a reviewer is likely to spend the minimum amount of time possible. Given that, make sure they use that time the way you want them to.

• Send out small chunks at a time, if possible. You are much more likely to get a deep review on a single topic than on 10 topics, or an entire manual. Figure out a way to sequence the process so that the reviewers have only a single, small task ahead of them at any given time.

• Use your organization's standard engineering tools and processes to promote your reviews. For example, in an Agile environment, use the sprint planning process to identify reviewers and reserve their time. Similarly, use the same tracking tools that the engineers use, such as JIRA, to track the reviews. You can enter review information and receive comments through the tool. This often works particularly well, because developers tend to rely strongly on those tools for their workflows. If you do not have a separate ticket open for your work documenting a feature, then use the feature's ticket to track the review. If you have the flexibility and opportunity to do so, write your content in the same environment that the developers write their code, so that reviews become just another pull request.

Enter the fray

- Set a firm deadline, at most one week from the time that you send the document out. There's rarely any point in setting a longer review period. If the reviewer doesn't get back to you within the first 24 hours, then you will get the review on the day of the deadline, or the day after the deadline, if at all.

- Send out a reminder about a day before the review is due. Send out additional reminders after the due date, if necessary. Don't allow more than a two or three-day grace period, however, without escalating the matter in some way.

- Negotiate. If a reviewer hasn't completed their review on time, talk to them and find out why. Agree on a new date that they can commit to.

- Keep the pressure on. If you haven't received a quality review in the allotted time, that's a problem. You need to make sure that it is not just your problem. If you are working in an Agile environment, use the scrum process and workflow to raise your issue.

- Public shaming. Feel free to bring the matter of reviews gone missing to the attention of the entire team. Use email follow-ups, team meetings, and so on. This is not you berating anyone. This is you getting your job done.

- Be realistic. If you send the material to an engineer, a product manager, a support person, and a writer, be content if you get one thorough review, provided that review comes from the engineer. You can always chat with the product manager to resolve the need for use case review. With the support person, all you can do is try your best and let the chips fall where they will (unless the support team was a key agitator for the feature, in which case, make sure that they review the documentation). With the other writer...well, writers are usually exceedingly prompt in their reviews.

- Escalate if necessary. Work with project managers, engineering managers, QA managers, and so on, when necessary, to ensure that your review needs get met.
- Track reviews assiduously.

After the dust settles

- Review each review. Not all reviewers do a good job on their reviews. Nevertheless, it is your responsibility to ensure that your documentation is accurate, so you need to ensure that the reviews are thorough. If you suspect that a reviewer did a hasty job, find a way to get the review you need anyway. Talk to them. Ask for clarification on a particular section, for example. Or send the material out to another reviewer with equivalent skills, if there is one. For example, perhaps there's another engineer who also understands the feature. Or try one of the other techniques covered here: review meetings, public shaming, and so on. Also, consider that there might be a good reason that they didn't do a proper review. Maybe they're the wrong reviewer for the material. Maybe they're not confident of their language skills. Maybe they're up against a series of deadlines and cannot really focus their mind on your review for a few more weeks. Investigate, negotiate, develop the relationship, solve the problem. You're a tech writer, that's what you do.
- Hold a review meeting, if necessary. These meetings can be valuable, but should generally be used only after you have attempted to get written reviews and either haven't gotten the reviews or have gotten conflicting reviews. Make sure that the reviewers have read the material before the meeting. If they haven't, end the meeting immediately and reschedule it. Review meetings can be particularly useful if there are differences of

opinion among reviewers. When you hold a review meeting, project the material on a screen. Allow plenty of time for the meeting, and go through the material line-by-line. If the entire reason for the meeting is that you haven't been able to otherwise get feedback on your material, then do your best to make the experience relatively painful and laborious (it usually will be, in any case), so that the next time that you need something reviewed, those reviewers have extra motivation to submit their comments on time.

A necessary caution

Tempting as it is, never offer reviewers cookies or other bribes. The tendency among some writers to, essentially, plead for reviews as if they were asking for something over and beyond the norm of the reviewers' responsibilities is unprofessional, unseemly, and counter-productive. It inevitably makes the review process more difficult in the future for both the writer and the other writers on your team.

Think of what you are communicating when you start going down this route. First, it puts you in a relationship of submission to your reviewers. You do not want to adopt the role of supplicant. It will get you nowhere. A review request must be understood as a request between equals. Second, rather than understanding their role in, and responsibility for, ensuring documentation quality, the reviewers begin to see their reviews as favors to be bartered. This is not a sustainable, healthy, or workable relationship, and it will torpedo the efforts of the entire department.

If you're great at making cookies, offer them at some time entirely unrelated to the review process, so that it is clear that you are not establishing any sort of quid pro quo.

Finally

Never give up. Jump up and down, if necessary. Do not release your documentation without sufficient review, no matter what.

Bear in mind that if a customer runs into a problem when using the documentation, you are going to get the blame. And deservedly so, if you have short-circuited the review process.

QA and technical verification

QA team members are a great source for reviews of all your technical material. They typically have a deep understanding of the feature and have written test cases that reflect the likely usage of the code. They can also help your efforts in many other ways. For example, they can:

- Explain odd aspects of a feature's behavior. QA is a great source for information. They often understand the behavior of a feature better than the developers.

- Loan you a test environment.

- Review your documentation. They often pick up on feature idiosyncrasies, such as edge cases, that the other reviewers miss.

- Most importantly, the QA team can test your procedures.

For reviews of procedures, formal QA is indispensable. QA team members can subject your procedures to rigorous and objective testing.

You do not need to submit all your procedures for formal QA. If the procedure is simple and easy for you to test yourself, for example, by viewing the results, then you probably don't need to involve QA. More complex and difficult procedures, however, benefit tremendously from formal testing.

Whether you submit a procedure for QA depends on its complexity, its potential for wreaking havoc, and the relative difficulty of adequately testing it yourself. These are some characteristics of procedures that benefit from formal QA:

- Complex, multi-step procedures.

- Procedures that can alter data or potentially lead to loss of data or other harm.

- Procedures that require a significant commitment from the customer in time or resources.

- Procedures whose nature requires a testing environment that is difficult to set up on your own.
- Procedures where it is difficult to fully confirm their success or failure.
- Procedures that have the potential for failure in edge cases.

As with any review, having someone else test your procedures can uncover unstated assumptions, missing steps, and so on, that will trip up your customers. So you might consider requesting formal QA even for procedures that you feel you can adequately test yourself.

Examples of procedures that strongly benefit from formal testing include migration and upgrade procedures, procedures that transform data, and procedures that fix unstable systems.

These are some of the reasons to involve QA in procedure testing:

- QA is well equipped to test procedures. For example, if you create a procedure that involves multiple, distributed instances of your software, the QA team already has test environments that can replicate your needs. Or if you create a migration procedure that deals with some odd issue that only occurs with certain versions, they can easily spin up all those versions.
- QA knows what to look for. After they run the procedure and it seems to succeed, they can run tests to make sure the system is actually working as it should. They know how and where to probe the system. They are good at testing for edge cases and other issues that might otherwise go unnoticed.
- QA is already testing the features that you're writing about, so they usually can test your procedures without much extra effort on their part, as they already have the test beds set up and they are following related test cases.
- As a corollary, when the QA team is testing new features, they should test against the customer documentation whenever possible, rather than against the engineering documents. If the

feature works one way but the docs say that it works some other way, that's as much of a problem as the feature not working at all.

The key point to remember is this: QA team members are experts at finding problems. They do this all the time with the code, and they can, and should, do it with your documentation.

When working with QA:

- Integrate your requests into the standard QA process. Testing procedures should not be something extra that happens outside the code QA. As with the code, so with docs: formal validation is a requirement for release.

- Be specific. Indicate exactly what procedures you want them to test and include any other relevant information.

- Request the testing at the right time in the development cycle. Not only should your documentation be in close-to-final form, but the code should be complete as well.

- Get written confirmation of test completion and results. This establishes accountability and provides a paper trail if the procedure later fails for a customer. That way, you can then improve the process for testing your procedures.

15. Tools and Content Delivery

When it comes to choosing a content delivery tool or authoring platform, it should come as no surprise that there is no such thing as a one-size-fits-all solution. A former colleague who recently joined a software startup was assigned to establish new product documentation and set up a doc team. He asked, "Can you recommend a good tool for writing and publishing docs?" The only realistic answer is: "Nope." There is no way to recommend a specific content delivery tool, authoring platform, or content management system without knowing a pile of information about what the information deliverables need to do and how a doc team intends to operate. There are a great many variables that feed into the decision about the technologies you use to write, edit, publish, and maintain your documentation. Unless you are privileged enough to have a clear strategy, a bucket of money, and answers to all your questions, you're going to have to evaluate your needs and find a best-fit solution in the open source or commercial marketplace.

To frame this discussion a little bit, this chapter is divided according to broad categories for consideration. Each category offers some insight into what out-of-the box solutions might provide. None of the information is exhaustive—someone is probably coding The Next Big Thing in doc authoring at this very moment—and all of it is colored by opinions and experiences researching and implementing doc tools in real life. If you are trying to make a thoughtful choice about adopting a documentation platform, hopefully this chapter will provide some framework to help you make a decision.

Unless called out separately, the terms "documentation platform" or "documentation tool" refer to the combined functionality provided by content management, content delivery, and content authoring tools.

Content management and delivery

Broadly speaking, this category encompasses considerations about how to manage and control your documentation set and how you want to deliver your content to readers. This spans a broad range of variables, to say the least. Let's break it down.

For content management, ask yourself some questions about how you and your team intend to manage content.

- Will multiple people create and edit content? If yes, how does the tool manage source control? In other words, how does it ensure that two people are not trying to work on the same material at the same time?
- How will you manage versions of a document? How will the tool ensure that an author is working on the most up-to-date version of a document?
- How will you manage versions of a product? If you are writing about on-premises software, for example, you will likely need to maintain the product documentation for several versions of the product that are available to users. How does the tool ensure that readers can discover and access the right documentation for the version of the product they are using?
- If the documentation is online, how does the tool notify readers that new or updated content is available? Is that necessary?
- Does the tool offer any archiving or backup and restore capabilities?

For content management of your documentation, you might consider using Git. While it is not a documentation tool, Git manages source control of code, so in the same way that it manages and controls access to files that contain code, it can control files that contain documentation. If you're looking for fancy formatting capabilities and snazzy interfaces, Git will fall short of your needs. But if you need something clean and straightforward that will masterfully manage the written contributions of many authors, Git is an eminently viable solution. You can use it effectively with a lightweight markup language and a static site generator to create a viable documentation site. It will also keep your content close to the code, and by using it, you will rely the same workflow for review and commitment of changes that your developers use every day.

For content delivery, ask yourself some questions about how you intend to deliver the documentation to your customers.

- Will the content be primarily available online or offline, on the Web or in a printed or static format?
- If online, will you need to offer a mechanism for your readers to access it when they are offline?
- Does the tool ensure that images, tables, and other formatting elements remain intact and usable when converted from online to offline format?
- Does the tool make it obvious to users that they are accessing the right documentation for the product (and product version) they are using?
- Does the tool enable you to publish one article at a time, or are you only able to publish sets of material?

One could include "does it need to be mobile accessible" as a question, but see it under "Reader usability" in this chapter.

If you anticipate publishing materials in print or another static format, you might consider a desktop publishing tool like FrameMaker, or even Microsoft Word. Most tech writers will read that sentence and scoff, "MS Word?! Are you serious?" but depending on your needs, it can be a viable solution. The point is to try to anticipate the form your documentation will take, then choose a tool that meets those needs without a bunch of excess functionality. There's no point in spending a fortune setting up a robust documentation and community knowledgebase solution if all you want to do is include a printed booklet of instructions with your product.

Authoring usability

The things to consider in this category might be the most
intuitive or easiest to answer. These are the things you need to
think about in terms of how you and your team will create and edit
your product's documentation.

- Does the tool enable writers to draft content that remains
inaccessible by readers until ready for publication?

- If your team is authoring online in a web app environment,
does the tool auto-save or otherwise prevent loss of work?

- Can authors easily compare versions of their content?

- Can authors revert to an earlier version of their work?

- Does the tool offer any kind of workflow management? For
example, can an author write content, then send it to an editor or
subject matter expert to review so that they can make notes and
send it back to the author for revision before publication?

- Will you be authoring content in a structured format, such as
DITA? If so, does the tool support and enforce structured
authoring?

- How important is WYSIWYG authoring to your writers and
editors? Will they be comfortable writing in markdown, wiki
markup, or XML, or is it important for them to prepare content
using an interface that displays the material with all its formatting
visible?

- How does the system manage linking between articles or doc
sets?

- Does the tool facilitate content reuse? How well would that
content reuse mechanism scale?

With the right set of requirements, you might consider using a
wiki or an online publication tool like Wordpress. Easy to use, they
offer interfaces that favor WYSIWYG content creation and
multiple authors, and they enable quick publication of completed
material. Out-of-the-box, these tools generally don't facilitate the
writing of drafts beyond a simple "save for later," or let you
manage multiple versions of content to match multiple versions of

a product. They certainly do not enforce structured authoring or facilitate workflow management for creating content. However, if it's important that you enable many people to author content and your team favors flexibility and quick publication, such a tool could prove quite reasonable.

If your organization favors collaboration and reusability of content, you could consider a larger-scale, commercial solution such as MindTouch or Madcap Flare. If you intend to have people in multiple departments contribute to your company's written publications in various formats, such as Support creating knowledge base articles and Marketing creating white papers alongside the product documentation that you create, this could be a good solution.

If you have significant requirements for content reuse and localization, then a DITA-based XML content management system from a company like IXIASOFT or Vasont might be the best fit.

And as we said before, using markdown in Git, to stay close to the code, or Microsoft Word, for small-scale printed documentation, might be the best match for your requirements.

Remember that you can apply the principles of structured authoring in any information development environment. Don't let a documentation tool dictate how you design and develop your information. Start with the combined requirements of customers and your own internal needs, and choose the tool that fulfills them most efficiently at the lowest cost.

Reader usability

Arguably, the most important things to consider stem from the experience your customers will have with your product documentation. Assuming you are doing some form of electronic delivery, put in the effort to deliver a clean, responsive design and pay attention to how well searching works.

- If online, does your documentation display nicely in multiple browsers on multiple operating systems?

- If converted from online to offline, does the formatting "stick" so that a reader can still see all the content?
- Is the documentation interface universally accessible?
- What is the reader's experience searching for information in your documentation? If offline, are the index, table of contents, and glossary thoughtfully structured? If online, does the search mechanism organically yield relevant results? Or does it operate based upon manually identified keywords?
- Does the tool facilitate localization of content? In other words, if you anticipate translating your content from, say, a roman alphabet to a Cyrillic one, will the tool be able to display it?
- Will your readers often access the documentation from a mobile device? How gracefully does the tool present information on small screens?
- Does the tool support reader interaction? Is there a way for a reader to leave comments, ask questions, or access other resources for help? (This leads to the related question of how you intend to manage your customer interactions. See Chapter 5, "Customer Feedback.")

Documentation metrics and SEO

You should also consider what you want to track in terms of productivity, return on investment, and readership of your online documentation.

- Does the tool offer any capability to track a user's experience with the documentation, such as the series of articles they viewed?
- Does the tool ensure that changing a page title does not change the URL, which might result in broken links for users or loss of SEO "juice"?
- What other metrics might you want to examine for, say, ROI of writer effort, and how might the tool facilitate gathering such data?

The truth is, as long as your documentation tool doesn't egregiously break links, you can probably use a host of other tools for measuring reader interaction with the content. For example, Google Analytics offers valuable information about page hits, bounce rate, time on page, customer demographics, user flow, and more, all of which can inform an analysis of customer usage. A content management platform will also provide some internal metrics about topic reuse and authoring, and such a capability might be a data point to consider when making your decision.

Integration and support

If you are reading this chapter because you are trying to decide on a solution to replace your existing documentation tool, consider how well the solution will work with other software and processes you have in place. Further, consider the support you have within your organization for setting up, maintaining, extending, and troubleshooting issues with your documentation tool.

- Is it feasible to transfer your existing content in its existing format to the platform? Would a migration of material involve multiple steps to manipulate the format?

- How much information redesign will the adoption of the new tool require?

- How much training will the writers need to use it?

- Thinking ahead, does the format of the documentation tool lock you in to the tool forever? Will the format make it nearly impossible to move to another tool in the future?

- How extensible is the tool? Does it offer community-built or vendor-built plug-ins or other extensions? Does the tool facilitate you building your own extensions or customizations?

- Who on your team or in your organization has the skills and bandwidth to be able to help you set up and maintain the tool? Are you on your own with the out-of-the-box solution, or is there a person or team who can help you with customizations and extensions?

For these considerations, it matters less which tool you choose. The important thing is whether you have the skill set, or access to someone with the skill set, to configure and manage the solution. If you are largely on your own, choose a simple tool that lets you focus on the writing and publication of content, rather than a flashier tool with fancy user interactions or more complex functionality. After all, the most important thing is that your readers have access to the information they need to do their jobs.

In the interest of future-proofing, you would be ill-advised to select a tool that uses a highly specialized or proprietary data format that might make future migrations nearly impossible. If you are starting afresh with product documentation, hedge your bets by choosing a tool that uses a data format that is highly portable and reasonably usable by both machines and humans, such as XML or a lightweight markup language.

Pricing

Arguably, this will be the most clear-cut of your considerations: how much money do you have to spend on a documentation platform? For open source technologies, the price is certainly right, but it comes with the cost of limited technical support and a lot of DIY effort. This is not necessarily a bad thing since it potentially gives you, the product documentation owner, a lot of leeway in how you use and extend your tool. Generally speaking, an open source tool is likely to have broader flexibility in terms of data format, integration with other software, extensibility, and portability.

Alternatively, a commercial solution might be more purpose-built for a particular market group, industry, or publication format. If that suits your needs, then a commercial solution that relies on an established schema might make your job of producing documentation, or collaborating to produce documentation, much easier than an open source tool. Carefully consider any training costs, monthly subscriptions, or maintenance fees associated with a documentation platform because it can result in a low ROI if your team uses only a fraction of the available features.

Beyond these considerations, there is one last question to ask yourself if you are thinking about switching to a new platform: for the problems you perceive, is the cause really the tool you're using, or is it the process? It might be both. But if your processes are broken, a new tool will not solve them. In fact, it might make them worse. Before you start looking for a tool to solve all your problems with product documentation, take a hard look at the authoring, editing, and publication processes you have in place. Resolve what you can by correcting processes first, then set about choosing a tool that will meet the needs of functional, rather than dysfunctional, processes.

If there is truly nothing out there that meets your needs, no combination of tools that could possibly do the job, you could consider building something new. The effort to get it off the ground will be considerably greater and likely much more expensive, but it's not inconceivable that your needs might best be met by a custom documentation platform.

Ultimately, when it comes to evaluating documentation platforms, begin with the end in mind. Use the considerations in this chapter as the beginning of a checklist of functional requirements, but do not start evaluating tools until you have a clear set of prioritized goals. Think about the experience you want your readers to have and that you want your authors to have, and write down those experiences. Then write functional requirements that feed those experiences. It is easy to become excited by amazing features and grand functionality, but beware about biting off far more than you need to chew. Don't overthink it. The goal is to deliver useful words to your customers. Choose the simplest method of doing so.

Wiki-based documentation: a case study

The documentation team at Splunk consists of about 40 people, including writers, editors, and managers. We write all the customer-facing documentation for the entire suite of software products that our company develops. Further, we are tasked with providing documentation for our developer community to enable them to write applications that extend the Splunk platform.

We started more than a decade ago with a few community-minded folks who bravely took on the task of preparing instructions for our initial customers. These first content contributors were creative, irreverent, and open-minded. Here, open-minded has three meanings: open in the sense of collaboration and community inclusion; open in the sense of loose demands for consistent style or structure; and open in the sense of open-source software. The attributes we valued (and continue to value) were scrappiness, creativity, innovation, and openness. The team didn't have budget for fancy authoring software, but they knew that contributions had to come from all employee groups, they wanted publication to be instantaneous, and that Splunk documentation should be publicly available on the web, because the product is available for free. The company started with a wiki because everyone knew how to use it, and it fulfilled the other delivery requirements.

To be candid, the decision at the time was less about weighing the pros and cons of a broad spectrum of tools, or considering what the needs might be ten years down the road; it was more about fulfilling immediate requirements while holding true to the company principles. The adoption of the wiki was expedient, effective, and a good fit for the Splunk culture.

Our documentation platform is a customization of MediaWiki that we call Ponydocs. It is available as open source. The main customizations are:

- Support for multiple products and versions

- Branching and inheriting of topics for multiple products and versions
- On-the-fly PDF generation
- Topic-based feedback
- Semantic URLS
- Importing static HTML
- Banners
- Per-product permissions

The Internet has a lot to say about documentation using a wiki. For every good thing that a wiki does, someone is quick to point out where a wiki falls short. Without addressing every criticism, it is worth examining several common ones and how we use Ponydocs to overcome some standard wiki shortcomings.

Managing content in a collaborative authoring environment

At Splunk, all employees can edit the documentation. When we mention that to many tech writers, they look a little pale and shaky. Perhaps they are imagining a management directive handed down to them: "We're a collaborative company! Just imagine how up-to-the minute our product documentation will be! Anyone can add content so surely everyone will contribute!" They entertain fearful thoughts of chaotic information architecture, duplicate content, circular logic, long-winded diatribes in the form of Knowledge Articles, and a manifest ignorance of the finer points of grammar and clear writing. Further, this anxiety extends into what has been referred to as Content ROT (redundant, obsolete, and trivial). If everyone owns content creation, then no one owns it, right? And if no one owns it, no one will validate it, update it, curate it, or kill it when necessary.

The reality, at least at Splunk, is far less alarming. The vast majority of our colleagues rarely edit or add words. Those who do make only minor changes and corrections. Why? Partly, it is because the company knows that there is a whole team of professionals dedicated to developing, confirming, and delivering documentation. It is also true that a relatively small number of employees possess the technical knowledge to make meaningful changes to the documentation. In some cases, it is just not a priority for other employees to update the documentation. In others, it is because people feel ill-qualified or intimidated to contribute to something that all our customers can see as soon as the page is saved. A mistake would be public and highly visible. But they needn't worry: the tech writers are watching.

The doc team uses an RSS feed that monitors all changes to our entire content set. No single person on the documentation team is responsible for monitoring that RSS feed and tuning up any content that folks add or adjust, but we all organically keep an eye on things. Writers can also use the MediaWiki "Watch page" feature for the topics they own. These features provide a safety net for both our tech writers and our other contributors: the writers have the comfort of oversight and authority over what goes into the docs they own, and our contributors know that if they don't use the right terminology or adhere to the rules of grammar, a writer will quickly and quietly adjust the contribution. The exposure and risk are smaller than people imagine.

As we grow beyond a company of 4000 employees, this approach might not scale. And when it ceases to work, we will adapt. But for now, what we observe is that the growth in the company has resulted in a *decrease* in the number of contributors from outside the doc team, not an increase at all. The curve seems more logarithmic than exponential or linear.

We encourage those knowledgeable and intrepid colleagues who do contribute, who boldly step in to update or correct our documentation. They dive into documentation because they care, because they want our content to be relevant, up-to-date, and valuable. They are taking ownership of the quality of our company's documentation and the customer experience. We encourage our colleagues to keep reading, using, contributing to, and correcting our product documentation; it is everyone's responsibility to give our customers an excellent experience.

Link management

The concern about maintaining hyperlinks in wikis is not unfounded. 404s are common, and perhaps wikis are more susceptible to the problem because hard-coding and collaboration don't work well together. In other words, if one author hard-codes a link to another topic, or sub-heading in a topic, and someone else edits the content of the destination topic in such a way that it changes the URL, you have created an instant (and largely silent) failure. In fact, every time you edit a topic heading, you might risk breaking dozens of hyperlinks that point to that topic. MediaWiki does not provide any dynamic link updating, although other wikis such as Confluence do. True content management systems also have a variety of mechanisms for link management.

We rely on a MediaWiki tool that an author can use to display a list of all the incoming links to the topic they are editing. When we must reorganize content in a way that would break incoming links, we can identify what it will break and fix it. We also accept that broken links happen, and address it by running reports to find and clean them up on a regular basis.

Markup instead of visual editing

For writers accustomed to WYSIWYG editing, the constraints of using wiki markup to create documentation can be irritating. Complex tables are particularly difficult. But as with any markup language, using wiki markup separates content from presentation. The ability to rely on style sheets to deliver the visual design of your information provides powerful freedom and flexibility. Writers concentrate on information design without the distraction of adjusting layout and other settings derived from desktop publishing.

Supporting a customized wiki

As with any authoring and delivery system, developer support is crucial. Ponydocs is a living, breathing product that requires constant care and feeding. We regularly require improvements, changes, and adaptations of functionality as well as bug fixes. For this, we rely on web developers in our IT Business Applications team. Without people working to maintain, update, and improve Ponydocs, it would not be viable as an authoring and publication tool.

Because open-source software is the foundation of Ponydocs, we can also enhance our platform using extensions and customizations from the broader developer community to address our needs. Our in-house developers provide any necessary customization, but for many features, we do not need to start from scratch.

Integrating wiki content with other systems

Out of the box, a wiki might not lend itself well to integrating with other systems. Atlassian's product line integrates Confluence, their wiki solution, with JIRA, their issue-tracking software and other Atlassian offerings. At Splunk, we have extended Ponydocs to integrate with other systems as well.

- Context-sensitive help links within Splunk software look up the relevant Splunk documentation topic using MediaWiki tagging.

- Known issues and fixed problems lists in Splunk release notes are automatically generated from JIRA and rendered as MediaWiki pages using a custom extension.

- The Splunk documentation site searches and displays the content of Splunk Answers, our community forum. Each page correlates its primary heading with the title of an Answers post to assemble and present a list of "Related Answers" in a sidebar.

Supporting multiple product versions

One of the main features of Ponydocs is that it allows readers to view documentation for a specific version of the product they are using. This is a significant customization of plain MediaWiki, and is one of the original features of Ponydocs. Because it incorporates versioning, Ponydocs also enables writers to branch or inherit topics or entire documentation sets from one release to another. In other words, there is built-in functionality to "inherit forward" all the written material for version 2.1.1, for example, to version 2.1.2. Then, a writer can branch specific topics in the 2.1.2 version to reflect the changes and additions specific to that release.

Creating PDFs

Ponydocs supports creating PDFs on the fly, either for an entire manual or a specific topic. Although Splunk content is optimized for viewing on the web, many thousands of customers download PDF files every month, so this is an important feature to maintain.

Content reuse

Where DITA handles this well, wiki-based documentation does not. The need to reuse or include a particular article, or portion of an article, in another one is not something that a wiki manages gracefully. MediaWiki does have template and transclusion features for complete pages and named sections. Our release notes automation system relies on this feature, and we have built an additional capability in Ponydocs to enable topics to display for more than one product. Customers who use our Splunk Cloud service rely on a lot of the same user information that our on-premises Splunk Enterprise customers need. We can display the same topic for each customer, in the context of their own product. This content reuse capability is not very granular, but it delivers the fundamentals and we continue to work with our web development team to improve it so that it meets more refined use cases.

16. Working with Customer Support

The relationship between documentation and customer support is mutually valuable. A successful, ongoing collaboration between these two teams can have demonstrable impact on customer satisfaction and the company's financial performance.

Why work with Customer Support?

Collaborating with Support can give you greater insight into the customer experience, which in turn, improves your documentation. It also lends weight to your voice as a customer advocate on your scrum team. At Splunk, Support and Documentation were part of the same organization for several years, and we have worked hard to maintain the active relationship we established during that time.

Support teams receive a high volume of cases that provide a perspective on customer pain points. For example, reviewing Support cases can help you identify frequently missed details or setup procedures that are more difficult in real life than in a test environment. The feedback that comes from real-life use cases gives development teams more perspective on what the customers want and need.

Support engineers know how to make things work from end to end, and they can highlight difficult points that a development team might not have foreseen. Support engineers see real-world systems that consist of diverse features interacting with each other.

Support engineers can also be good reviewers for documentation covering feature enhancements, particularly if they have been supporting that part of the product for a while.

It's not all a one-way street. Improved documentation can help with Support case deflection. See Chapter 10, "Measuring Success." In addition, documentation can help cases that aren't deflected by giving customers a basic head start with troubleshooting. Writers embedded in a scrum team can alert Support of possible problems in upcoming products, or tip them off about hard questions they should be asking the dev team in signoff meetings. Working with Support promotes an alliance on the voice of customers. Support engineers address customer questions and concerns, and serve as experts in the products that their company manufactures and develops. As writers, we can advocate on Support's behalf from within the products organization. We can object to product design decisions that will make the product hard to support, we can advocate for better error messaging, and we can make sure that each scrum team trains Support on a new feature.

Minimizing any specialized Support knowledge base, and putting as much content into the official documentation as you can, reduces confusion for the customer. Imagine having a question and having two or more separate places to find the answer. It also helps your docs if Support uses them and gives you feedback when they don't work for them. There will always be information that Support needs to capture that is too specific for the general product documentation, such as runbooks or troubleshooting steps that involve details about a customer environment. An internal wiki or knowledge base is an important resource for this type of information. But the first head of Support at Splunk took the stance that "the docs are the knowledge base." To the greatest possible degree, we have continued on that path, and our customers have thanked us for it. Bear in mind that to follow this path, you must ensure that the documentation answers real questions and issues that customers encounter.

How to work with technical support engineers

When working with Support engineers, make it as easy as possible for them to work with you. Support engineers work in a different environment from most writers. They see customers at their most frustrated, and each support engineer typically has a high volume of cases to close under significant time pressure.

Be respectful of their time, and make sure they know you are doing so. Generally, doc reviews are difficult to fit into a Support engineer's schedule, but face-to-face working meetings with well-defined agendas can be a useful way to get information. Come prepared for this meeting, and demonstrate that you have gotten some work done in preparation for their input. Be sure you search any Support or community knowledge base. Make yourself available for their requests. Maintain a physical presence near the Support team, if possible. At Splunk, writers sometimes work for an hour or two at a visitor desk in the Support department. Participate in your company's support community (Support chat room, Answers forum, user group chat). When Support gets trained on a new feature, listen to the questions they ask the products team. Attend issue review meetings with Support engineers. Help Support ask development teams the tough questions as early as possible.

Some companies offer employees a chance to participate in a "support rotation." Support rotations give employees the opportunity to spend time learning the tricks and strategies of troubleshooting the product that Support has acquired and developed over the product's lifetime. The support rotation affords participants the opportunity to learn diagnostic and repair strategies that might be more difficult to discover from working only with a development team. Most importantly for writers, and for writers working with Support, it exposes you to the customer frustration that Support witnesses every day.

Splunk Support holds a weekly "Top Issues" meeting that is heavily attended by the documentation team and occasionally attended by sustaining engineers. Support engineers report issues with the product, ask for help, and offer suggestions for improvement. The documentation team reports on doc improvements that they've completed or need help with.

All employees can edit Splunk documentation. Support contributes directly to documentation by adding items to release notes and by making minor technical corrections when they encounter them.

Support sometimes helps a writer, especially a new writer, answer customer feedback. At the bottom of every documentation topic on docs.splunk.com is a "Was this topic useful?" form. The writer responsible for the content is also responsible for replying to this customer feedback and incorporating any enhancements that result from this interaction. Support is an excellent resource for a new writer in answering customer feedback questions, and for helping define the distinction between how involved a question can be before requiring the customer to open a Support case.

Support engineers also sometimes help create new documentation on existing features. In one example at Splunk, a writer identified a group of four Support engineers and set up a standing meeting every week. The meeting time was useful for reviewing doc work in progress and identifying and prioritizing future work.

Keep in mind that for both good and bad, Support engineers provide a perspective that is different from documentation, product managers, and developers. Support engineers are often the first people to witness problems in your product. As a result, they can be pessimistic about either the quality of your product or the possibility of improvement. Remember where they are coming from, and identify when a negative customer experience has affected their perspective. You might need to adjust your attitude accordingly. Quickly publishing incremental improvements to the docs can be a relief in this situation, and promote a positive working relationship with the Support engineers.

17. Working with Engineers

Many aspects of working with engineers are covered in other chapters in this book, including:

- 2, "Agile"
- 4, "Collaborative Authoring"
- 11, "Research for Technical Writers"
- 14, "Technical Verification"

This chapter focuses on your individual work with engineers, specifically discussing how to build a successful relationship and get the most out of the conversations you have with your engineering partners.

Technical writing is a relationship business, and it also has some things in common with investigative journalism: you must establish credibility, develop your sources, and understand the language of the subject you're writing about.

Your relationship with your subject matter experts is essential to your success. Many of these SMEs will be engineers. You might or might not have an engineering background yourself, but when in a writing role, you must understand the engineer's workflow, interests, and habits of mind. By doing so, you will increase the chances of getting the information you need and influencing the design and functioning of the product you document.

Obtain the right background

To be a good technical writer, you have to understand the mental model that your engineers have and speak the same language they use. No matter how well you understand the customer and the use case, if you lack the knowledge and technical skill to have a substantive, collaborative, *peer* conversation with engineers, you are going to be marginalized in the project team and the quality of your content will suffer. In the best case, you will turn into a copy editor who polishes what engineers give you. In the worst case, they will dismiss or ignore you entirely, and you will be forced to document something you don't understand without meaningful access to useful information from the people who built it.

So do your homework, look smart and cool and impress your friends! The good news is that almost any technical domain you need to learn has plentiful free resources available on the internet. From mainframes to edge computing, from COBOL to Scala, from semiconductors to storage appliances, if you apply yourself, you can develop the knowledge you need to have the right kind of conversations with engineers. Don't waste an engineer's time on something you can figure out yourself.

Prepare for the conversation

Over time, you will establish credibility and an individual relationship with the engineers you work with most frequently. You should still prepare for every substantive conversation. For one thing, it's just professional. For another, it will help focus the conversation and use everyone's time more efficiently.

Before you meet with engineers:

• Read any existing persona and use case information, requirements, specifications, and test plans.

• Familiarize yourself with the terminology, whether it is industry jargon, internal shorthand, or new terminology associated with the product you're working on.

Make the conversation worthwhile

Ideally, the entire cross-functional development team will have a shared understanding of what they are building, who they are building it for, and why. Confirming this is a good place to start. Use questions like:

• Why did we decide to build this?

• Who will use this?

• Why? What will they be trying to accomplish?

• How will it work? For example:

  o Will the customer configure this feature?

  o Is it extensible?

  o Does the product offer multiple ways to do the same thing?

Ask to see a demo. Also ask where you can get a build so you can play with the feature yourself.

Typically, engineers are working on a very narrow slice of the product. Use your broader knowledge of the overall workflow and customer scenarios to ask questions about dependencies with other components, interactions with other products, or variation within the technology stack. Exercise your own knowledge to help shape the product. If the product is docs and docs are the product, then you are a designer, a developer, and a product manager, too. Use that expertise to make the conversation worthwhile for the engineer and, ultimately, for the customer who will receive what you build together.

18. Working with Marketing

You have more in common with marketing than you might think. They are the people responsible for communicating the value of your product to an internal and external audience. The deliverables of a marketing team can be technical marketing (blog posts, tech briefs, white papers), social media marketing (tweets, Facebook posts, Instagram, and so on), and multimedia content like videos or podcasts. Marketing can also develop product demos for sales to use, manage the company presence at industry events such as conferences, and organize your own company's user conference.

By working with the marketing team, a documentation team or writer can gain a better understanding of the target customer, prepare for future changes to the product or the target market, and align the customer experience between marketing content and the product documentation.

How can marketing help docs

Ensure the doc team is informed about marketing priorities and feature naming

If you know what features marketing is focusing on for their sales plays, you can focus on getting the relevant content in the best shape, because it will be likely to get more attention at the time your product launches.

Share customer feedback and perspective

Marketing is responsible for knowing the target customers and creating a strategy to raise their awareness about your company's products. Just as you can learn from UX personas, you can learn from the target customer definitions that marketing has identified. In addition, marketing may have a direct path to customer interaction through proof-of-concept demos, industry events, and other demand generation activities. If you have a good relationship with the marketing team, they can share some of the highlights or takeaways that might be relevant to docs. They might uncover procedures that confused the user, or awkward areas of the product where specific documentation can close a usability gap. Addressing real customer questions using real-world customer scenarios to enhance your documentation will make it more likely people will read and use your content, because it will be more relevant to them.

Understand the market players and how your competitors are documenting their products

For example, if competitors are focused on use cases or videos, you might get tapped to assist with that at your own company. In addition, if a feature in your product was built in response to a competitor's feature, they might have documentation or scenarios that you can read to identify opportunities for improvement or competitive advantage.

Align on customer goals

How do you expect people to use the product? What types of messaging is your company focusing on? If the messaging revolves around ease-of-use, and the docs emphasize complex scenarios and high-level content, customers will be less likely to try the product or read the documentation. Help translate the picture presented by marketing into reality with your documentation. Show your customer how they can do the things that marketing claims.

Understand future goals/roadmap plans

Think of how best to address future plans in the docs. Maybe the product will start to shift and become a platform that includes subsidiary content that could be versioned separately. Maybe your company is introducing bundled solutions. How will changes like these affect your information architecture? Maybe the product's customer demographic has evolved, and you should simplify or retarget your content to accommodate new and different customer populations. Working with marketing can help you prepare for changes like this, rather than reactively responding to a customer shift. Proactive, anticipatory changes that help welcome customers to the docs—and your products—are what you want to achieve.

Write better docs

Marketing content revolves around a call to action, driving the customer to do something (usually buy a product). Similar principles apply between marketing and technical documentation (see Steve Krug's *Don't Make Me Think*).[9] Know your audience. Figure out what you want them to learn and to do when they read your documentation. Write lean, action-oriented, goal-focused content that is relevant for specific customers doing specific things. Don't write more than you need to help someone solve their problem. Make the most important information easy to find on the page, and easy to search for on the web.

How docs can help marketing

Share, share, share. Marketing can benefit a lot from what you know and what you write. You can share:

- Your knowledge of what customers seem to find helpful. If you get doc feedback, you have a line of customer insight that isn't flowing to the marketing team.
- Workflows that could be easily leveraged as marketing content. If the product is doing a particularly good job addressing a customer scenario, make sure marketing knows about it.

---

[9] *Don't Make Me Think: A Common Sense Approach to Web Usability*, Second Edition, Steve Krug, New Riders, 2005.

- Your content. The information you develop might help marketing get a bit more technical and below-the-surface of the features, so they can adapt some scenario-driven content from the docs to highlight product capabilities in a more tangible way.
- Your writing skills. Be willing to edit or write content cross-functionally. If your marketing team doesn't have content marketing expertise, you can help develop some blog or white paper content for the marketing team. This will get you closer to their view of customers and build the collaborative relationship.
- Your product knowledge. Help marketing improve the relevance of their content and the overall story the company tells about its products. Provide guidance on feature naming, or historical aspects of the product, or feedback about what might confuse customers.

Especially for time-strapped marketing teams, partnering with the documentation team can help them produce higher-quality content in a shorter timeframe by basing it on the relevant technical documentation.

Get started working with marketing

If marketing is already involved with the planning and release process, and you know who your marketing representative is, reach out to them over email or in person and suggest getting lunch to discuss options. You can also set up a meeting or send an email proposal.

Depending on the culture of your company, as well as the needs and availability of team members, you can set up regular meetings, or perhaps just work to establish the communication channels via email and keep in touch. In large companies, it's not likely that you work on the same floor as the marketing team, let alone the same building or city, so do your best to break down the silos and forge a partnership. If you're not sure who your marketing peer is, or if you have dedicated marketing people for the product, work with product management or the project manager to get in touch with them and explain how you can help each other.

Social media marketing

You can bolster your company's social media presence by providing well-written topics for marketing to highlight. You might have a lot of content that is primarily reference-oriented, but scenario-based information aligns well with a marketing focus. Using channels like social media can be a great avenue for bringing users to your docs.

If your doc team has its own social media accounts, even better. Managing your social media content directly is a great way to reach customers and build your own brand within the larger presence of the company. Use some more casual language (helpful if the tech writing voice can feel stifling at times) and direct users to the #newhotness of your #product with a tweet. Highlight scenarios and use cases with blog posts and stories on Twitter or Instagram. Share fixed bugs and snippets from the release notes to encourage people to upgrade to the latest version and make it clear that your documentation team responds to customer feedback.

Developing an integrated content experience

The users of your product will usually get their first introduction to product features from marketing or other pre-sales content. As a documentation team, you want their transition from the marketing content to the documentation content to be seamless, cohesive, and logical. Make sure that you and the marketing team align your content to the product priorities. If you must focus on "minimum viable docs" to be ready at release time, focus on the product features that marketing will emphasize. Work with marketing to make sure you are aligned on feature naming. You can also work together with the marketing team so that their descriptions of product capabilities are technically accurate.

The Product is Docs

When it comes to developing scenario-based and use-case-driven documentation, marketing often has demo content and workflows that they present to customers. Write content to match these scenarios, so that customers can see the same story reflected with a new level of detail as they learn more about the product. You're guiding the customer from the marketing pitch of "here's what you can do with our product" to the documentation level of "here are the specifics of how you do this with our product."

Think about content from marketing and docs as the guide that holds your customer's hand as they reach a buying decision, then purchase your product, then start using it, then recommend it to others. You don't want customers to be disoriented or, worse, feel misled. Customers want you to guide their experience and help them get their job done. Creating an integrated content experience through a cross-functional partnership helps build trust in your company and products, and makes your customers more productive with your products faster because they understand the value of what they have bought and how it applies directly to the problems they need to solve.

Where the partnership fits in a release cycle

Where and when you work with marketing depends on the development or release cycles that each of your teams follow. Ideally, you will stay in touch with marketing throughout the entire development and release cycle and include them as a stakeholder in your documentation.

- Involve marketing *before you write your documentation* to find out what features or deliverables they plan to focus on in their marketing plan.

- Involve marketing *as you start writing* to validate feature and product names.

- Involve marketing in the review or sign-off process *after you write your documentation* to validate your treatment of the use cases and your links to related information.

You will likely find that staying in touch with marketing on a strategic level makes sense in the early stages of a release cycle, and that the month before release, you can partner on more tactical level to coordinate priorities and the specifics of what you are delivering.

How to improve your relationship with the marketing team

If you've tried to work with marketing before and been burned, here are some tips.

- Ensure clear responsibilities and boundaries.
- Don't sacrifice technical accuracy to produce shinier content.
- Focus on relevance and influence your marketing colleagues to do the same.
- Work with product management or other functions that partner closely with marketing to gain trust and explain the benefits of working together.
- Help out at industry events that the marketing team plans. Everyone appreciates a volunteer, and you will benefit by meeting customers and demonstrating your product knowledge.

19. Working with Product Management

All product managers are different, but there seems to be one universally shared trait: they are too busy to do everything they need to do. How well a tech writer works with their PM can make all the difference in achieving a successful outcome for the documentation and the product as a whole.

How product management can help docs

Define use cases, user stories, and acceptance criteria

Part of the core responsibility of a product manager is to understand customers and to translate their business needs into product goals. As a result, PMs are the only member of the product team who should be writing user stories and articulating the use cases for your products and features. In a high-functioning team, your PMs might be writing both user stories and use cases without being prompted, but in other cases the technical writer needs to coax or actively elicit them.

If, despite your repeated encouragement, your PMs are not defining complete user stories, you have a process problem and should engage with your program manager (if you have one) as well as your PM to figure out how to address this need. It is helpful, in this case, to demonstrate how the lack of user stories with acceptance criteria affects the entire team: designers, developers, testers, writers. Even if your developers and QA colleagues are not flagging this as an issue, you can probably demonstrate how a particular feature went awry due to lack of shared understanding of what you were building and why. As a writer, you are well-positioned to craft this message so that everyone on the team understands the impact and is motivated to push for improvement.

If your PMs are not able to articulate use cases for your product when asked, you have a product problem. While there are circumstances under which your team might want to iteratively release a cutting-edge product that doesn't yet have a strongly expressed market need, your PM should still be able to describe a use case. If they truly cannot, it's time to consider raising a blocker issue. If the use case is tentative, you can use that information to make good decisions about how much time you should spend crafting your content in this iteration. Perhaps less is more, and you can spend your time on other projects while this idea matures.

Set clear priorities for the product as a whole

For a team to function well, product management must define priorities and ensure the entire team understands them. In any healthy product team, no one would disagree with this statement. However, day-to-day demands can overcome this shared acknowledgement, and people can forget to focus on team-wide clarity and the accessibility of these priorities. If anyone on the team expresses confusion or disagreement about the priorities, you can champion the PM's efforts to update the priorities where they are written down, or help write them if that has not yet happened. Unless the high-level priorities exist in writing, they might as well not exist, and you and your colleagues should keep asking for them. The overall product priorities help you define the scope of your documentation and the kinds of content that might be required, and thus to prioritize your learning objectives for your docs.

Even if each product team has clearly written and accessible priorities, if you are the writer for multiple scrum teams, you might still struggle to balance competing priorities between teams. This can be awkward if your PMs are not closely aligned within their own functional team. When you find yourself in the position of having to sort out your own documentation priorities among competing product or feature teams, the safest strategy is to model good priority-setting behavior. Articulate your criteria, make the resulting priorities and tradeoffs clearly available to all stakeholders, and then be consistent about holding to both criteria and priorities. How you go about setting your criteria can vary widely based on your organization. You might use customer feedback, companywide strategic goals, release deadlines, or an evaluation of which team's user stories have acceptance criteria defined first. Ideally, your PMs will react to your priorities by improving their own functional team collaboration so that they can take back the burden of prioritizing efforts across teams, leaving technical writers free to concentrate their efforts on developing excellent content rather than prioritizing projects.

Review and approve a doc plan

Chapter 8, "Learning Objectives," discusses writing learning objectives as a way to scope documentation work and get buy-in on a plan before writing begins. But how do you get a product manager to look at your learning objectives and give you the feedback you need? Or, what if you have multiple PMs sharing the ownership of the product and you cannot get input from them all? Communication, once again, is key. If you have multiple PMs, identify one PM as your point person for documentation questions. Perhaps you will be lucky enough that your PMs identify that person for you, but otherwise you might just have to choose the PM that is most willing and able to collaborate with documentation as your primary stakeholder.

To get the early attention that you need on your doc plan, pay attention to your PM's preferred communication style. Do they want to read something offline and respond in their own time? Do they want a ticket assigned to them for review? Do they want a meeting? Unless they strongly prefer not to meet, consider meeting briefly with your PM the first time that you write a doc plan for one of their projects so that you can introduce your learning objectives and explain how they will translate into written documentation. This one-on-one can help PMs more efficiently and effectively evaluate your learning objectives in future iterations or for other projects, without requiring a meeting. Note also that learning objectives are an excellent tool to refine stories and use cases. Reviewing and discussing documentation plans can be an illuminating exercise for product managers. Demonstrate that value to them as you go through this review process.

Review and approve content for publication

Product management sign-off on docs is as essential as product management sign-off on any other part of the product. Documentation, whether it is in-product help or external content, is an integral part of the product, and thus is part of the overall ownership responsibility of the product manager. If you think PM is not signing off on docs before publication, think again! Silence implies consent, even if that silence is the result of a compacted or broken process. Even if PM did not review docs at all before publication, their product ownership burden extends to any misalignment between the documentation and the overall product delivery. To relieve this burden and ensure proper alignment, make it as easy as possible for the PM to review and sign off on docs. That could mean supporting a better process by highlighting the gaps and suggesting improvement ideas. It might mean using your existing process more effectively to make this review and sign off a clearly articulated pre-release step. Or it could mean using the personal relationship you have developed with your team to insist on the review that you need.

How docs can help product management

Validate product management's understanding of the primary audience

If your PM is defining a product aimed at one audience, they expect that the technical writer will design their docs with the same audience in mind. Validate your audience assumptions with your PM during your initial doc planning to avoid frustration later. A particularly effective way to ensure you share your idea of your audience with your PM is to develop use case and scenario-based documentation, and use learning objectives to refine what you are developing and why. See Chapter 8, "Learning Objectives."

Pinpoint what areas in docs most need product management review

Some PMs love to read all your docs in detail, but PMs who have the time to do that are rare. Don't send them your entire doc and ask them to review it. Also, don't ask your PM the same questions you have asked engineers and testers, unless a collaborative answer is required. Instead, call out the exact areas that most require PM attention. Let your earlier agreement about audience and approach carry the rest of the load. So, which areas in your docs most merit your PM's attention? Consider asking your PM to review any navigation topics, as well as use cases and scenario-driven documentation. Depending on the nature of your product, your PM might also need to be closely involved in the release notes, including the new features, known issues, and fixed problems lists.

Make it as easy as possible for product management to give feedback

Just as with engineers, adapt your review style to match your PM. Ask them about their preferred methods of providing feedback and allow them to try out a few if they aren't sure. Depending on the tool you are using to deliver documentation, your PMs might be able to comment in-line or on a PDF, which saves them time because the comments can be immediately correlated to the location in the docs where they apply. If you are doing docs in Git, and they are comfortable using the Git review workflow, that can work well. You can open a ticket and have them comment through your ticket tracking system. If electronic review is not possible, you can offer to meet and take notes as they review the docs and react out loud. With this approach, the PM does not need to take the time to compose their comments formally in writing.

Don't sulk if you don't get any feedback. Reevaluate your methods, clarify what you are asking for, and try again. Talk to the product manager about the mutual benefits of attending to documentation and share some of the customer feedback they should know about.

Get involved early in the development process

PM and docs can work most effectively together when you embed yourself as completely as you can with your team as early as possible in the product development cycle. Early involvement allows you to gain a deeper understanding of how your product works, but—much more importantly—it exposes you to the "why" early enough to ask questions about the business case for your product or features. Observe as your PM articulates the why to your team and see your development team responds with the "how." Early involvement also allows you to write in-product text and error messages as features develop, and to work closely with PM and UX to test and improve usability and workflow in the product at each iteration.

Try to get your hands on the product at the same time that the PM does, so that you can maintain a shared understanding of how it evolves, and no one has to bring you up to speed late in the project cycle. Staying informed about all the details of your product is your responsibility as the tech writer, so if something isn't clear you need to identify your SME and ask for the clarity you need. Don't expect to achieve the same level of synergy with your PM if you only begin working actively on documentation at the very end of the development cycle.

Raise issues promptly

Rely on your own expertise about what users will find confusing and be confident when you raise issues about product design and definition. You are another voice on the team that is accustomed to articulating the perspective and needs of the user. Of course, it will be the PM that decides which of the perceived problems are worth tackling and which are not.

File tickets or pull requests to change "small" UX issues early rather than assuming they will get cleaned up later or that someone will ask your advice. Don't restrict your attention to in-product wording of UI text and error messages; also attend to issues like consistency in styling, product and feature terminology, capitalization, punctuation, and color. PMs often lack the time to attend to this level of detail, especially in earlier design stages, but by prioritizing this throughout the development process you can avoid mistakes or pernicious style issues getting baked into the final build.

If something is blocking your work and the PM can unblock you, don't be shy about telling them and then reminding them if they need a reminder. A PM hates to be the bottleneck and the blocker of any team member's progress. Phrasing your blocker as "You can unblock me by doing XYZ" can help them act fast to make the decision or provide the information you need most efficiently.

Champion efficiency

Create standards, processes, and templates for your team whenever doing so will improve efficiency. If you notice the team is struggling with a similar issue repeatedly, perhaps you can work with your PM to investigate the issue, define a best practice around it, and document that in a central location. Then, whenever the best practice fails to fully meet the team's needs, update it so that it evolves with the team.

Look for ways to apply feedback, goals, and preferences from your PM across multiple features, releases, or products; not just the specific case you were asking about one time. PMs are just like anyone else, in that they find it annoying to have to repeat themselves. Preserve their time so that they can give you feedback on the next item you need, not something they have covered with you already.

Share customer feedback

PMs want to be able to base their decisions on the most accurate possible view of who the customer is and what their pain points are. If you have a robust method for gathering feedback from customers through your doc site, find a way to make the results available to your PM team so they can consider it in conjunction with their other field sources. The feedback you receive on docs might not accurately represent the opinions of users as a whole. For example, perhaps more of your new users leave feedback than your experienced users. But the data can be an excellent source of information for your PMs as they make product decisions, especially if they see trends that suggest the audience demographic is changing over time, or that the customer needs and use of the product are evolving.

What a healthy PM/Docs partnership can look like

Technical writers and product managers share the same high-level goals. Both are focused on customer satisfaction and success. Both want a high-quality product that solves real customer problems. Both are heavily invested in a smoothly functioning team.

Technical writers can draw upon the goals and perspectives they share with product management. Each can rely upon the other to contribute different strengths or areas of focus. Often, a PM sets the strategy and works hard to articulate a vision and big picture goals. Similarly, it is the tech writer's job to understand all the details. Just as a PM's sense of high-level priorities can help tech writers avoid unnecessary distractions, a tech writer can flag bugs or UX issues that might otherwise have passed under the radar of a busy PM.

Similarly, your PM might be more closely aligned with some functional teams (executive staff, sales, marketing, support), and you are more aligned with others (UX, QA, engineering.) Who is more closely aligned with what group varies by team, but you can support PM by sharing cross-functional information. Tech writers also tend to be organized and good at thinking about processes, so you are well-situated to support and improve your team's processes as part of your daily work, which enables a PM to spend less energy fighting to reduce friction. This support is especially helpful to a PM leading a team without the help of a PMO resource.

Finally, the docs team and the PM team share a central perspective in a products organization. Technical writers and product managers operate as a hub, maintaining good relationships and clear lines of communication with all other functional teams and with external customers. Both can understand and promote the perspectives of all other team members and share the responsibility to advocate for customers so that they can be successful and productive with your products.

20. Working with Remote Teams

Many software companies with headquarters in the U.S. have engineering teams in other countries, such as China, India, Russia, or Israel. As a technical writer in the home office, working with a remote engineering or scrum team presents many challenges. The engineers who are developing and testing the products you are charged with documenting are living and working on the other side of the world—many, many time zones away. You can't just walk over and say "Al, show me how this thing works." Not only are you separated by time zones, you are separated by language and cultural differences.

Process, Process, Process

Process is always important, but even more important when working with a distributed/remote team. It is important to have a well-defined development lifecycle, milestones, and hand-offs. If the entire product development team—project managers, product managers, solution architects, software developers, QA engineers, UX designers, technical writers—works in the same office, you still need process, but you can get away with a little sloppiness… hallway conversations, informal discussions, and so on. But when your team is distributed, you can't just casually check in with someone to ask if they finished their task because when you're working, they're sleeping, and when they're working, you're sleeping.

Agile and remote teams

The Agile Manifesto (http://agilemanifesto.org) says: "The most efficient and effective method of conveying information to and within a development team is face-to-face conversation." Can the members of a team divided between North America and Asia or Eastern Europe have efficient and effective daily standups? Fundamentally, no. This is a big hindrance. When you are physically separated, well-defined handoff criteria are necessary. The definition of done becomes an essential collaboration tool. Suggestions for working with a remote engineering team:

- Frequent checkpoints or milestones. The milestones should be directly tied to the backlog story the team is working on.
- Demos of the product. Live demos with screen sharing are best, but if the time zones or technology prevent it, have the team record videos of the demos and put them in a shared location.
- Formal handoffs. Formal handoffs may not seem very Agile, but it is absolutely necessary to have formal handoffs when you are working with a remote team. For example, one team at Splunk established a formal handoff between the Solution Architect and the lead engineer to signal the beginning of product development, and a formal handoff from development to QA and Docs when the product reached feature complete.
- Document all product changes in your issue tracking system. Hallway conversations can't transmit to the whole team. Similarly, the distribution of any specific email or chat conversation might not include the whole team, and is certainly not available to people who join the team later, or are part of a dependent team. It is very important to put everything that affects a release in your tracking system so that the changes and reasons behind those changes are captured and all team members, including the documentation writers, have access to the information.
- Your issue tracking software should be the source of truth. Every team member must be diligent in keeping it up to date so that it reflects the current reality. Any team member should be able to look at an Agile board and get an accurate picture of the state of the project. If a member starts work on a ticket, they need to indicate that progress has started on the ticket. When work is finished on a ticket, the status needs to be set to Resolved. Not only does this give an accurate picture of progress in the sprint, it is very important for managing dependencies.

- Require user stories. User stories give the context. They provide the business reason for an application or feature and help the entire team understand how the product or feature is going to be used and what problem it solves for the customer. If your product manager has not provided well-considered user stories, ask for them. See Chapter 19, "Working with Product Management" for more about this.

Communication, communication, communication

With so little opportunity for meetings that involve team members in different time zones, written communication becomes even more important. In addition to using your issue tracking system as a true collaboration platform, create some lightweight, practical templates to ensure the easy capture and transmission of essential development information.

Face to face time

Know that even though you are an exemplary communicator, you might not pick up all the information you need if you are the one working remotely. Make sure that you remind your team members that you are remote and that if there's anything they need to share with you, to make sure to do so over available communication media.

If you can, schedule office visits from time to time to let people know that you do, in fact, still work there. Face time reinforces connections with the team that you just can't get using conferencing tools.

You also might be separated by language and cultural differences. When you are working internationally, it is even more important to meet each other face to face. Here is the story of one writer:

> *When I first joined the team and was participating in meetings with the remote engineering team, I could not*

understand the engineers on the phone call due to their heavily accented English (because our meetings are held early in the morning in their time zone and not all of them are in the office at that time, we do not use video conferencing). But everyone else in the conference room with me was nodding and comprehending and able to identify the different speakers. I thought this was some kind of magic. How were they doing this? I was hopelessly lost. I could understand so little. When I traveled to the remote office and met the team members in person, this all changed. Now I could put faces to names. Speaking to the team members in person I was able to follow what they were saying better. I gradually got used to their accents and way of speaking. Now, when I'm on the phone in San Francisco talking to them, I can usually identify who is speaking and picture their face and my comprehension is much better. Knowing you are working with a real person instead of just a name is also very important.

Some teams might not have the budget for travel. How do you establish rapport with remote engineers? When you are on the phone with remote team members, you don't have body language or visual cues to help you understand. One way to establish rapport is to ask about local holidays or traditions. Show interest in their culture. You can ask about their kids or pets or their vacation or travel plans. Since English is not their first language, many developers in other countries prefer to communicate in writing. Use online chat, email, or a wiki to keep the conversation going.

Use video conferencing if possible. If you do not use video conferencing, is important for the project manager or the person leading the meeting to give every team or team member a chance to speak or give their status and for each speaker to identify themselves before speaking. The delay in international calls causes a lot of talking over each other and false starts. You need a project manager who can lead the meetings and ask each team member to speak in turn. If the scrum team is too large to do this, it should be broken down into smaller scrum teams. This also aids in sprint planning and overall team effectiveness.

Out of site, out of mind

If you are a writer working with a distributed development team, it is really important to maintain visibility and cultivate a relationship with everyone as a member of the team. At first, engineers might view the tech writing role as a hindrance when you are asking a lot of questions from overseas, but after they see the value you add, they will start to treat you as a full-fledged member of the team and will proactively inform you about changes to the product, issues that need to be documented, UI text they'd like you to review, and so on. Be involved as early in the product development cycle as possible. If you are asking engineers to correct UI text in the last phase of the product development cycle, they see that as having to go back to redo a task they thought was finished. If you work with them when they are developing the UI, the team can get it right the first time. Make yourself as visible and vocal as you need to be to have equal footing with everyone else in the room, even if that room is virtual.

When you are a remote team member, you still need to be seen and heard by the team members who are not remote. You also need to have a lot of patience with those members who might not pay attention to you because you are not in the office all the time. Being a remote team member requires a high level of availability and visibility. Out of sight is out of mind, so you need to make sure that others on your team are always aware of your presence. You can accomplish this in several ways:

- Frequent emails and other forms of communication.
- Frequent participation in issue tracking systems. Make sure that you track *all* your work. If you use a ticketing system like JIRA, make sure all the work you do is associated with a ticket. Learn how to use the program and work with the project manager

to get your tickets assigned and linked to epics, stories, or other tickets.

- A high level of communication with managers and project managers. When you participate remotely in an Agile/scrum environment, communication with the project manager is essential. Attend all stand-ups, even if they might not necessarily apply to you. Attend all scrum review and planning meetings, even if you have nothing to show in a review (but always try to have something to demo—it's better!).

Do your best to facilitate communication with your teammates. As you work with teammates and reinforce your virtual presence, those teammates will be less likely to forget about your physical absence from the office.

Meet your deadlines

Probably the most important thing that you need to consider when you work remotely is that the deadlines that you, your manager, or your team set are important. If you miss a deadline, it looks bad and separates you from your teammates. Make sure you make enough time for yourself to finish all tasks assigned to you. You can leave some of wiggle room to ensure that your most critical tasks get done either on time or early, and don't be afraid to defer projects that aren't critical to the team's mission.

Deal with conference calls and increase your presence in meetings

By nature, conference calls are distributed forms of communication: many people dial into a conference bridge, have a meeting, then scatter (often to another meeting which invariably has another conference call). You can help facilitate your presence even when you work remotely by having access to your own conference bridge and screen sharing. This lets you schedule a conference call quickly and have others join in if no others can do so.

If you can, use videoconferencing to host your meetings. Encourage team members to use it as well. If you don't have videoconferencing installed in your conference rooms, you might need to get permission from your manager to set up a "roving" laptop with a microphone and camera whose sole purpose is to wheel around to meeting rooms.

When you are in a meeting, don't just sit quietly. If you have opinions, no matter how small, speak up. If you are on a conference call and you have nothing to offer, consider whether you should be on that call in the first place, or if your time would be better spent working on that project that's due tomorrow.

Support your team as much as possible

Make sure you support your on-site teams as much as possible. Go the extra mile. Check in with your teammates to confirm that they have everything they need from you. Don't be afraid to check in repeatedly with several members of each team. If they know that you are there to help them with what's important in their work, they are more likely to help you with what's important to yours. The team succeeds together.

21. Working with User Experience and Design

"Working as designed." That's a phrase that you might know well as a technical writer. It's the standard line that engineers and product managers offer when they determine that a bug filed against their product is in fact not a deficiency at all, but the way it's supposed to work. That thing that doesn't seem to be working right? It's okay, don't worry about it. We meant for it to do that. If you're worried that customers will be confused by it, we can explain it with some inline text or just put in help links to the documentation. Problem solved! Doc around it!

If you have spent any time working as a technical writer, you have probably run into a variety of versions of this scenario— features with strange functionality and weird design issues, workflows that seem to be missing steps, cryptic field labeling, and so on. One way of dealing with this as a writer is to document the product as is—write text that helps people over the functional hurdles and guides them to a satisfactory ending. But this isn't the best approach. Customers will come to resent the reading they have to do simply in order to understand how the product wants them to work, and in the long run it enables poor UX practices.

The fact is, sometimes our UX design and engineering teams turn out products that fail the customer, even when they're functioning exactly "as designed." Sometimes that design is flawed, or based on assumptions—about who the customer is, about how the feature should work, about the design principles guiding the project—that need to be challenged. And sometimes the designers just aren't thinking things through, operating with a "good enough" mindset.

As one designer used to say, some UX teams end up designing products "from the inside out, rather than the outside in." As part of the Agile process, designers are given a set of feature requirements by the product manager, and they then create a design that meets those requirements with precision. Sometimes the design they come up with is elegant, even beautiful by engineering standards, and reflect all the current trends in UX design. But the thing they create might not actually work for the audience that will use it. Your designers might be checking all the boxes they have for their design principles, but they're not actually thinking of the people they're designing for.

But you are. You're a tech writer, and you have to think about how people use your product, because you have to explain it to them and make it comprehensible.

If you see something, say something: the writer's role as user advocate

As a technical writer, you are accustomed to thinking about the product you document from the perspective of the user. What aspects of the product will they intuitively understand? What aspects will they require help with? If you begin from this position, you can see the places where your product design is lacking. How? Well, anytime you find yourself having to do extra work to explain how something works, you might be facing a problem that is less about you and your explanatory abilities than it is about the broken UX of the feature you're describing.

Your position as the "first user" of a new product or feature could be somewhat unique among your development team. Product managers, UX designers, and engineers can all find themselves building features that somehow leave the product audience out of the picture, perhaps not entirely, but in a myriad of small ways. But your only question is: how do I help the audience for this product understand it?

Also, if you work in a feature-driven Agile development environment, you are likely to have a bigger picture view of your product because you work across multiple scrum teams. You see how all the parts fit together, and you can easily see the parts that don't.

You have a right to question imperfect design. Not all writers realize this, and in some cases they might be discouraged from doing so. Don't let yourself be excluded from design discussions. Rebut any vague "too many cooks in the kitchen" arguments. Find out where the design prototypes are and file tasks against the people responsible to fix poorly considered UX choices. When you know something should be fixed, you have to speak up.

UX issues get harder to fix the longer you wait. It's best if you can catch them early on during the design phase, before they're committed to code. You won't be able to catch everything, and issues will find their way to the code, but beware of letting them go for too long, because they have a way of getting "baked into" the product. This is especially true of bad terminology—you can remove it from the UI, but if it's still in the code, the wrong terms will be resurrected by engineers who spend more time staring at the code that runs your product than working hands-on with the product itself.

Fixing issues during the design phase can make things easier for your engineers as well. It's easier to file bugs against concepts than it is to file bugs against code. If you can work with your UX designers while they are in the design phase of your development project, you can head off bad ideas before they become entrenched problems down the line. Ideally, you'll be able to create a working relationship that benefits everyone—especially your customers. If your UX designers and engineers can see that you're not creating drama for the sake of creating drama and actually have their interests at heart, your work as a UX fixer will earn you respect.

If the problems originate from incomplete or poorly-defined requirements, docs and UX can be powerful collaborators and insist on a clearer understanding of what the team is building and why.

UX issues and how to identify them

There's a software design adage that every technical writer knows by heart, mainly because other people in the industry drop it on them like it's a Heretofore Unrevealed Universal Truth: "If a product is designed correctly, it shouldn't need any documentation." Our minds are expected to be blown by this statement, but any tech writer who's been around the block a few times just nods sagely and agrees. Because it's true. Our jobs wouldn't be necessary if all software applications were as simple to use as a mobile phone app. But they're not, and until some especially brilliant UX minds figure out a way to reduce their complexity to that level, we're still on the payroll.

The truth of that shopworn saying is often your first clue that something's not right in Designland: if you assess a new feature and feel that you're going to have to expend a significantly large number of words to explain it to the audience that the feature is being designed for, there could be some UX issues in there that need illumination. These issues can range from the relatively simple (terminology, field labeling) to the complex (feature workflow, overall design).

Confusing terminology

Have you ever documented a feature and found yourself having to explain that a [odd term for a thing] is actually a [much more familiar term for a thing] in order to get the concept across to customers? That's likely a sign that [much more familiar term for a thing] is the term they should have used in the first place. For example, if an accepted term for a concept throughout your product is "field," why should it be acceptable to refer to it as an "attribute" in a new feature? The moment you find yourself thinking about writing a sentence like "An 'attribute' is essentially what we refer to as a 'field' elsewhere in this product," you know that something is broken.

Other terminology issues to watch out for:

- Overloaded terms—when you find yourself having to deal with five completely different kinds of "objects" in your product (for example).
- Vague terminology – what does "object" really tell someone anyway?
- Slippery identities—when a concept in your design has different names depending on where it appears in the product. For example, you could have an item that shows up as a "Saved Search" in a "Saved Searches" list and as a "Security Report" in a "Security Reports" list. What is it? What will best inform the customer to help them use the product as a whole?
- Needless resurrection of dead terminology—as mentioned in the previous section, this is something that can happen when names for things are captured in the code long after they're removed from the UI.
- Placeholder terms that are never fixed—when people put something in with the intention to loop back and fix it at a later date…but don't.

Terminology battles can be surprisingly exhausting, mainly because terms are as tenacious as viruses—you can extinguish them in one area only to find them pop up in another, months later. Choose your battles carefully, and keep the overall value of the product to the customer in mind.

Mysterious interactions

Occasionally UX teams deliver software designs that include—or in the worst cases, hinge upon—an assumption that users will either "get" some sort of mysterious interaction, or that they won't care to know what is going on behind the scenes. This often comes up with "magic button" solutions, where clicking a button causes a variety of things to happen invisibly in order to achieve a particular result. When you see something like this, take some time to question whether users will be satisfied with this black box approach.

- Is there a chance that they will need to troubleshoot the hidden processes? If the promised result is incorrect, do users have a way to fix it?
- Can the feature add a significant amount of processing overhead to the product? If so, do users have a method to manage it? If they can't manage it, are there at least warning messages that this might be the case?
- Are there conditions under which the feature does not work, or that it is not available? Are these conditions adequately clear to the user?
- Is there appropriate error messaging for the feature, or has that been minimized as well?

As you study the implementation of "mysterious interaction" features, an obvious red flag would be if you realize that, in order to properly support the feature, you need to write a lot of documentation to explain how it works, the details that users need to know about when they use it, and the options they have to manage or control it, if any exist. Consider that some customers will never consult the documentation for seemingly simple features and UX interactions. To help them, encourage your UX designers to implement user assistance strategies that dispel some of the mystery around the feature.

Here are UX solutions you can consider:

- Minimal inline text in the UI to help users better understand what a feature does, possibly with links to the documentation.
- Clearly written error messages that explain what has gone wrong and how to solve the error condition.
- Additional management pages that provide important metrics about what is happening in the background and give users tools to identify and fix invalid results.

Progressively disclosing complexity is a solid principle for design as well as information development. Most customers in most situations might not need additional troubleshooting or management capabilities for a feature. But for the minority that do, documentation should not be the only part of the product that helps them.

Needlessly reinventing the wheel

If you are a veteran employee at your company, you might occasionally find yourself working with a development team that unwittingly puts in a lot of time designing a solution to a user story that has already been handled in a more elegant manner elsewhere in the product. This typically happens when the engineers and UX designers are relatively new and do not have a thorough understanding their product's functionality and how users typically interact with it.

Use your broader knowledge of how the whole product fits together to eliminate redundancy, and use your experience with customers to ensure that the best of the redundant solutions becomes the standard.

Over-reliance on user assistance

While you might be tempted to cram your product full of in-product user assistance, it's important to realize that adding a lot of text to the product does not mitigate poor design. Get the workflow right so you don't need as many words to explain it to customers.

Getting Involved

To be able to advocate for the best user experience possible, it's important to understand the problem that a software product is trying to solve, and how specifically a software design solution proposes to address the problem. To gain this level of insight, it's essential to get involved in the product design process at the earliest stage possible.

Speak to your product manager and UX designer during the requirements definition phase. Make sure they understand that as the team's technical writer, your goals are fully aligned with their goals, and that your perspective and feedback are key components in developing an intuitive and highly integrated user experience. Help them create an experience that does not rely on documentation as an abstract reference, but provides seamless guidance—pathways, prompts, clues, tips, definitions, and easy access to deep knowledge—all integrated from the beginning of the development process.

Arrange with your team to include you in product design meetings from the earliest stages forward, and make sure you contribute your perspective freely in those meetings. Speaking your mind will help you develop a constructive working relationship with the UX team. This rapport can prove invaluable in helping you advocate for the user on design issues as the product development process approaches deadlines and people come under the inevitable real-world pressures of delivering a functional product to market.

Make sure to read and review PRDs, wireframes, workflow diagrams, mock-ups, and demos; and listen to the feedback provided during real user testing.

UX design workshops

One great way to get involved in a design project from the ground up, and to hone your understanding (and appreciation) of the UX design process, is to attend a UX design workshop. UX teams are some of the most innovative and creative groups in the software development field, and they have many tricks up their collective sleeves for generating product designs. One of the most popular and effective methods, which is not exclusive to the software industry, is the immersive deep-dive product design workshop.

These deep-dive workshops bring together constituents from across the software development organization into cross-functional teams with the goal of creating an entirely new product. Over a period of several days, and in an isolated environment, the teams work through exercises to help identify problems and articulate solutions. Each team then gets their hands dirty working together

192

through a process of brainstorming, sketching, mock-up, review, and revision, in order to develop a unique product solution. Finally, each team's UX designer translates the team's final product design into a working mock-up, which is then subject to real-world user testing and feedback.

In the end, this immersive workshop process yields product designs that incorporate the interests and objectives of all the constituent members on the team. For example, product managers and engineers build a product that meets the business goals of both the company and the customer, while UX designers and, you, the technical writer, work collaboratively to advocate for the optimal user experience.

22. Afterword and Acknowledgments

If you have read this book cover to cover: congratulations! You just completed a guided tour through the world of information development. We hope that it gave you a stronger sense of the truly cross-functional nature of your job, and what it really takes to deliver high-quality products in today's world.

If you dipped in and out of specific chapters that interested you: likewise, congratulations! You have used this book in exactly the way we intended, and we hope it was valuable for you.

You know how much we value feedback. If you have comments or questions about the book, we would love to hear from you. Email us at docteambook@splunk.com.

Splunkers past and present devoted significant amounts of their time to bring their knowledge and expertise to bear on this project. While they were producing world-class documentation, helping customers solve problems, participating in the Splunk community, and shaping every aspect of the company's products, they put in extra effort to contribute this book to the profession. They are truly an amazing team:

- Andrew Brown
- Tony Corman
- Jessie Evans
- Louise Galindo
- Mike Glauser
- Stephen Goodman
- Holly Jauch
- Jessica Law
- Andrea Longdon
- Sarah Moir
- Malcolm Moore
- Matt Ness

The Product is Docs

- Robin Pille
- Janet Revell
- Steven Roback
- Fiona Robinson
- Laura Stewart
- Matt Tevenan
- Jennifer Worthington

54136282R00110

Made in the USA
Middletown, DE
13 July 2019